TOMORROW STARTS TODAY

by

Arthur B. Rutledge

Cover design: Jimmie L. Hurst
Cover photography: Don Rutledge

$1.00

Introduction

The United States of America's Bicentennial is a time of challenge for every American. It is a time of gratitude for God's blessings upon our land in the past. It is a time for renewal of our spiritual and moral commitment as a people.

It is an appropriate time for Southern Baptists to take a fresh look at ourselves. We are no longer a regional denomination. During the past 35 years Southern Baptists have become a national body. Cooperative Southern Baptist churches are more dispersed—now in all 50 states—than our spiritual forebears could have dreamed. The assignment of the Home Mission Board focuses on this nation—the 50 states and the territory of Puerto Rico.

What does the future hold? That's what this book is about. Southern Baptists' future witness and ministry will be determined to a considerable degree by their attitudes and commitments of today, as well as their willingness to face new challenges and opportunities with boldness. This book is an effort to interpret the changes of the immediate past and challenging opportunities ahead, and to suggest the thrust of Baptist home missions as the third century of our national life gets underway. It is likewise an effort to help each Christian find ways of furthering the cause of Christ throughout our homeland.

Whatever the future may hold, it is at hand. Tomorrow must build upon today. Tomorrow must start with the present. A poem by Ward Kaiser speaks to us in these lines:

Still the future speeds.
Tomorrow starts today.

People move, cities grow,
Things change.
In the name of God we must do better than before
The future will not wait.[1]

It may well be that our major Christian task at this juncture is to build new and stronger foundations of Christian faith and obedience in this nation. This is a necessity if we are to be strong as a nation and if our Christian witness around the world is to continue to be effective and to expand.

1

TWENTIETH CENTURY FRONTIERS

"With confused, empty people around us wherever we live, it is no longer possible to think of a mission field as somewhere off yonder."

If some modern-day Rip Van Winkle should wake from a sleep begun at the close of World War II he could not believe his eyes. Visits to the moon would boggle his mind. And he would find it even harder to believe that the world watched by way of television as men first walked on the moon.

He would discover that deaths from polio and pneumonia almost never occur in the United States and that malaria has been conquered. He would learn that progress is being made in the control and cure of cancer. And what would he think when someone told him of organ transplants?

As he looked for a job he would see that some persons now work four-day weeks and that almost everybody works shorter hours than a few years back. The size of salaries and the cost of goods and services would seem unreal. He would be puzzled by modern dress and hair fashions. He would be shocked by the open advertisements of X-rated movies. Widespread crimes of violence and large-scale drug abuse would stagger him. The active presence in America of "Eastern" religions would be a surprise.

We have always had change. What makes life so exciting, and sometimes so difficult at this point, is the rate of change. The changes of the past 30 years in American society have been more numerous and more dramatic than in all the previous 170 years of our national existence. The changes of the next 30 years are likely to be even greater. People who are concerned about the spiritual health of our nation and of the world need to listen, learn, plan and act.

The changes of the immediate past have placed before Christians a challenge of the first magnitude. And they point to some of the changes to be encountered as we begin the third century of our national life.

More People

Whenever Home Mission Board and Alaska Baptist leaders conferred during recent years, the oil pipeline and its opportunity of Christian witness have come up. The 789-mile-long pipeline will change Alaska, all the way from the oil deposits on the northern slope to the port city of Valdez on the south-central coast. At its peak the pipeline will carry 2 million barrels of crude oil a day from the Arctic to ice-free ports.

The pipeline will push the state's population forward by almost one third within a few years. It will spawn problems of housing and transportation, education and law enforcement.

Plans for missionary work were developed carefully. In mid-1974 the Home Mission Board joined the Alaska Baptist Convention in commissioning a missionary, James Eastland, to serve in oil worker camps along the pipeline route. Steps were taken to strengthen the existing work at key points and to begin new ministries in other towns along the pipeline.

The energy crunch has led also to exciting developments in Colorado, Utah and Wyoming, where oil can be extracted from shale in a 16,500-square-mile region. Two years ago two major oil companies leased 5,089 acres of this land from the federal government for 20 years at a cost of $210 million. Other tracts were scheduled for future leasing, and some lands were already in the hands of other oil companies. An enormous potential—enough oil to supply America's needs for more than 100 years—was locked up in these rocky mountain lands.

This development is expected to cause the population of three western Colorado counties to rise nearly fourfold by the 1980s—from 78,000 to 328,000. Similar increases will occur throughout the area. Some entirely new towns will be built. Here, as in Alaska, many social and moral problems—as well as outstanding opportunities for Christian missionary work—will arise.

The Home Mission Board has linked hands with the related state conventions in preparing for a Christ-honoring ministry and witness to the thousands of people expected in these areas. Population growth adds up to more needs and greater challenges to Southern Baptists and to all Christians.

Along with this movement of people will be a continuing increase in the national population. Some of this will come by the excess of births over deaths and some by immigration.

The United States has grown rapidly from slightly over 2 million in 1776 to beyond 212 million today.

In the early 1960s there were predictions that our national population would climb as high as 350 million by the year 2000. The guess has now dropped as low as 280 million, with not more than 250 million by 1985.

The slowdown in rate of growth during the past 10 years marks a change. Nevertheless there will be increases in all age brackets, with more than half of the gain coming among young adults ages 20 through 34. The 35-to-49 and the over-65 age groups are expected to register sizable gains also.

Since the settlement of the colonies on our eastern coast, our population has tended to move westward and slightly to the south. This was reflected again in the 1970 census and is expected to continue.

During the 1960s the western states had the largest percentage gain and the southern states had the largest total increase among the various regions. California, Florida, Texas and New York registered exceptional growth. Nevada had the largest percentage increase, followed by Arizona, Florida and Alaska.

The migration ahead is expected to follow the patterns of the past decade. People will move, in the main, toward the suburbs, toward coastal areas, toward urban regions, and toward areas offering a combination of moderate climate, available jobs and a variety of leisure time activities.

The field for Southern Baptists now encompasses the entire nation. The national population today is 10 times as large as when the Home Mission Board was established. More people mean heavier responsibilities and larger opportunities for the churches and their Home Mission Board. The home missions task is not diminishing; it is multiplying.

Growing Cities

Our population growth has centered in the cities. When the colonies banded together to form the United States, only 2 percent of their people lived in cities. It was an agricultural society.

We have now become an industrial nation, and the cities have mushroomed. In 1900, 42 percent of the American people lived in urban areas. The figure is now more than 70 percent. The rate of increase has slowed, but city population is still rising faster than the national growth rate.

If trends continue, according to some forecasters, more than half the people will be crowded into three giant "megalopolises" by the end of the century.

One will stretch from Boston to Washington (and some say as far south as Norfolk), another from Pittsburgh to Chicago, and a third from San Francisco to San Diego.

One writer commented: "It is this concentration of more and more people into a few urban areas, rather than the actual increase in the nation's population, that lies at the heart of most of our burgeoning social problems—soaring crime rates and violence, drug addiction, racial frictions, traffic strangulation."[2]

Cities furnish unique attractions. It is here that people find employment, entertainment and unusual educational and cultural opportunities. In addition many find the freedom to adopt a new lifestyle away from the close-knit home community. And it is in the cities that decisions affecting all areas of life are made. Banking and law, education and medicine, government and business come to their sharpest expression in the cities.

On the other hand cities have problems. They have problems of government and taxes, air and water pollution, secularism and poverty, lack of privacy and constant noise, violent crime and congested freeways.

An alternative to living in a crowded city is the new town. A recent report stated that 127 of these towns were either planned or already under construction. Their combined population will exceed 8 million. They present another challenge for Christian service.

But the central cities will not die. They appeal to people of many different lifestyles. The city's educational, vocational and marital opportunities make a strong pull on 18- to 24-year-olds. The central city is attractive to persons who want to live near their work. The increasing number of high-rise apartments and condominiums provide alternative housing opportunities.

The central cities, such as Washington, Atlanta, Dallas and Los Angeles, tend to have a high percentage of ethnic minority peoples. Often the older cities suffer fron severe blight in the inner city. It is in the hearts of these great cities that we find our worst ghettoes. Sub-standard housing and poverty or semi-poverty abound. Generally it is here that we find the needy aged. It is here that we most likely find people with strange lifestyles. The cities continue to have stable, one-family dwelling communities also, though some of these suffer from the ravages of time.

Southern Baptists must be aware of the city and must serve well there. We must find ways to serve effectively in high-rise apartments and in mobile home parks, in ghettoes and in suburbs, in urbanized rural communities and in new towns. A start has been made, and Baptists are deeply involved in ministering in the cities of our land.

The Rural Challenge

America enters its third century as an urbanized nation, but the rural population is holding its own. The number of full-time farm workers has dropped sharply during the past 25 years. The flight from the crowded cities, however, has brought many commuters, retirees and vacationers to the country.

Statistics show that most Southern Baptists are members of city churches. They reveal also that about two thirds of the denomination's churches are in the open country, villages or small towns. Most of us can name towns and villages that are drying up. A few hours' trip on practically any highway, excluding interstates, will take us through more than one small town with empty and run down business buildings. As the young move away for education or better financial opportunities, the future of churches in some smaller communities is in jeopardy.

In many rural areas, however, the opportunity is enlarging. The growing number of city people who have begun to move away from the noise and pressures of the big city to locate within commuting range of the metropolis provide this significant boost. Churches in resort areas, where throngs come to visit, fish, ski, or golf, face exciting new opportunities.

A 140-member rural church, near Oxford, North Carolina, is located near a public recreation area. Its community expands to 15,000 persons a day during the summer vacation season, and the church is involved in a Christian ministry to these visitors.

Other rural communities, especially those near a large city, have had mobile home parks developed in their communities recently. It is no longer true that occupants of such homes are more transient than the general population. These too constitute a growing opportunity for the rural church.

Most rural communities also have a large number of elderly people and poor people as well. They need loving attention. Rural youth may lack adequate recreational opportunities. The church can help greatly at all these points.

It could well be that one of the most fruitful opportunities for Christian witness and ministry will be in the less populous areas of our land, where access to people is easier. This can happen if churches are alert enough to understand the changes and flexible enough to develop programs to speak to people in their changed situation.

Missions on Today's Frontiers

Some exciting missions ministries are being carried on now on these "people frontiers."

The Metropolitan Frontier.—Wherever you travel in the cities of the United States you will almost certainly find Southern Baptists at work.

Across the southern states, where our roots are deepest and where the majority of our members live, Southern Baptists are the largest religious group in many cities. They are prominent in all the cities of the South, and our witness is strong and varied in such cosmopolitan centers as New Orleans, San Antonio, Miami and Baltimore.

9

There are less than a half dozen cities in the nation with a population over 50,000 without a Southern Baptist witness of some kind. Sometimes, as in New Haven, Connecticut, we serve in a joint project with other evangelicals. In cities like Denver and Detroit, where we have been active for 20 years or more, Southern Baptists have a strong base of churches, plus ministries among minority and disadvantaged persons.

About 15 years ago, the Home Mission Board focused on one large city each year, continuing this for several years. One of the first was Chicago. The Board designated $150,000 for what is called the "big cities" program in greater Chicago. With this money it purchased 10 church building sites and provided limited assistance on salaries for the pastors of the churches to be started at these points. These funds provided the impetus for 10 new congregations, including some of the strongest churches in metropolitan Chicago today. The list consists of Wheeling, Countryside, Des Plaines, Calumet City, Hoffman Estates, Elk Grove Village, Clarendon Hills, Palatine, Glenview and Skokie churches. As cities grow and costs rise it becomes increasingly difficult to establish enough needed churches. The years ahead surely will see home missions strategy calling for a vigorous push to strengthen our base for witness and ministry in key population centers.

The southern states were primary mission fields in the early years of Southern Baptist home mission work. Once again they are presenting demanding missionary and evangelistic calls. Because of the population turnover of the past 30 years, many cities of the South are having to grapple with problems which northern cities encountered much earlier.

We are moving away from the familiar situation in which the white Anglo-Saxon Protestant dominated the scene. Now in southern cities there is a wider variety of ethnic groups, religious movements and life patterns than ever before. The Bible Belt is changing at many points, and Southern Baptists are finding that southern cities are more difficult to minister to than ever before.

Enormous numbers of people, of all cultural levels and backgrounds, now live in apartments or condominiums. Some of these have chosen this to gain privacy. Others are there because they travel extensively. Whatever brings the people to apartments, it has not been easy to reach them for Christ and the church to any satisfying degree.

Some churches have provided apartments for lease. The First Chinese Baptist Church of San Francisco has constructed a 14-story building which includes four stories for worship and educational facilities and a home for the pastor, three stories for parking and seven stories of apartments for lease. Laypersons from the First Spanish Baptist Church of Atlanta rented an apartment house for subrental to international students who could not qualify to sign a normal rental lease. In each of these cases the sponsoring church will have excellent witnessing opportunities.

Home missionary-pastor Samuel G. Simpson and the Bronx Baptist Church have encouraged their members to locate in strategic places in multistory apartment buildings in metropolitan New York City. From these apartments they are seeking to open up opportunities for witnessing.

In addition to such approaches by mission congregations, several well-established Baptist churches have sponsored construction and operation of highrise homes for the aging. The list includes First Baptist Church of Orlando, Florida; Walnut Street Baptist Church of Louisville, Kentucky; South Hills Baptist Church of West Covina, California; and First

Baptist Church of Longview, Washington. Some churches have employed a staff minister to concentrate on work with apartment dwellers. Many home missionaries serve in fields where a high percentage of residents is apartment people. Mission action groups in the churches often get involved in ministries in apartments.

Home missionaries are encouraged to use every means available to reach apartment people. Avery and Myra Sayer serve in an apartment complex of LeFrak City, Queens, New York. The Home Mission Board provides a second apartment for them to use as a center for activities beamed toward residents. This enables the missionaries to offer day-care ministries, recreational and spiritual enrichment activities for young people, tutoring classes, Bible study, Vacation Bible School and Sunday chapel services. Small Bible study groups meet weekly or semimonthly in apartments. Such activities open doors for sharing the Christian faith with persons of ethnic backgrounds who otherwise might not be accessible to our witness.

All of our cities have slums. They have sections composed largely of people with irregular and inadequate income, people who are transient, and people who are neglected and in need of both spiritual and physical ministries. More than 250 home missionaries serve in just such settings, in cities all across the nation.

One such couple is Frank and Nancy Thomas, appointed to direct the Neighborhood Center in Albuquerque four years ago, immediately after their seminary graduation. With excellent staff and volunteer help, they schedule activities aimed at all segments of the community. These activities include pastoral ministries; a teen center; a well-child clinic; a drama project; a garden club; an athletic program; piano, guitar and voice lessons; a tutoring program

12

and a teen counseling group. Two dens of Cub Scouts meet in the Home Mission Board-owned building. The center has a cooperative relationship with the urban division of 4-H Clubs. In addition, sewing classes and self-improvement classes are offered, and assistance is given to delinquent youth.

Contemporary programs in our large cities are similar to those initiated over a half-century ago, but updated to appeal to people in their present circumstances. As cities grow, the need to update old approaches and develop creative new ways of serving will increase. The cities constitute our chief challenge.

The Board will almost surely accelerate the appointment of missionaries to serve in the cities and pour more of its resources into helping urban churches and associations respond to the pressing needs of these centers.

The rise of "new towns" presented a puzzling challenge. Virginia Baptists, through the Mount Vernon Association, established a church in Reston, Virginia, one of the first of the new cities.

The Denton County Baptist Association, assisted by the Texas state convention, bought the first land sold by the developers of Flower Mound, a new town in north Texas.

In other new towns, such as Columbia, Maryland, the only land and facilities available had to be secured in cooperation with other religious bodies, all using an interfaith religious center. James Hamblen was appointed by the Home Mission Board and the Baptist Convention of Maryland to direct Southern Baptist activities in Columbia. Six years ago this was a new kind of missionary service. Today Southern Baptists have a growing mission congregation in Columbia, served by John Woodall as mission pastor. Hamblen's duties have been enlarged to include service as new town consultant for Southern Baptists anywhere in the nation.

The Rural Frontier.—The Home Mission Board is committed to sending missionaries to meet specific needs. It is concerned also to help churches recognize and respond to the opportunities in their midst. The Board's staff includes specialists in many fields, whose major work is to help churches respond to their missions and evangelism needs.

Three years ago the Board's rural-urban missions program joined the church administration program of the Sunday School Board in conducting a national conference on the small church. This was the first time that Southern Baptists had ever held a national conference to help our smaller congregations.

The conference probed into the needs and opportunities of the small church, whether in city or country. More than 400 persons attended and found fresh information and inspiration to face the challenges of the small church in a changing America. The countryside is changing. These changes may complicate the situation for some rural churches, but they open up inspiring opportunities for others.

This is the case even in areas of limited change, such as Bolair, West Virginia, where Mark McAllister became the missionary pastor eight years ago.

Bolair Baptist Church is an open country church in Webster County, West Virginia. The county had a population of 9,300 and was isolated geographically and poor economically. Three fourths of the people received financial assistance from a government agency.

Church attendance was normally 15 to 20, with 30 a big crowd. The longest pastorate in the church's 10-year history had been 20 months. Two pastors stayed less than six months. The spirit of both the church and the community was depressing. The outlook for a fruitful ministry was bleak.

As Mark McAllister told the story in chapel at Southeastern Baptist Theological Seminary he said: "It seemed as though the people were oblivious to the needs. . . . It is at this point that we must develop an awareness. Awareness of needs and how to minister to those needs, but more importantly to minister to people."

He became aware that it would take more than mere invitations to church to reach any substantial portion of the three fourths of Webster County people who were without a church affiliation. He began working with youth, convinced that West Virginia's young people and not its coal were the state's leading natural resource. Sixty-three young people came to the parsonage for their first get-together. Soon the teenagers began to meet weekly for devotions, recreation and refreshment. The youth usually planned and conducted the devotions themselves. They named their gathering "The Peacemakers."

Parents began to show increasing interest. Church members came alive. People were won to Christ and baptized. Two young people surrendered to preach and another began to prepare for foreign mission work. The inspiring response of youth opened up new vistas of Christian service—to younger children, to the hard core poor and to unchurched areas nearby. A weekly between-Sundays meeting for children was started, with high attendance from the beginning.

The poor had special difficulties in travel, since the county had no bus or train service and many people were without cars. The church provided a twice-weekly transportation service to people of the entire county.

Bolair and three other churches initiated summer work camps in which church members reroofed a house and cut a year's supply of wood for families in need. The church began a weekly home Bible fellowship, attended by about 25. The church reached out to establish a mission in a town 45 miles away.

Other needs will still be met, such as tutoring, ministering to the lonely aged, and extension Vacation Bible Schools.

Mark McAllister said to the seminary audience that day, "Every church must have a multiple ministry, regardless of its size, its staff or its lack of personnel."

The spiritual frontiers of today come to sharpest focus in the cities. This is where most of the people live. It is here that we encounter more problems and more complex problems than ever before. More people, spreading cities and revitalized rural areas will add up to an exciting Christian opportunity as we enter the third century of our nation's life.

With confused, empty, disturbed people around us wherever we live, it is no longer possible to think of a mission field as somewhere off yonder. There are mission fields—in other parts of our land and all around the world—and there is such a field around each of us. People may flee the big cities for the quieter rural areas but the problems of the cities have invaded the country. Here too are drug abuse and alcoholism, crime and violence, family strain and illicit sex. The mission action emphasis of Woman's Missionary Union and Brotherhood has helped many churches discover and respond to new needs. The Home Mission Board has appointed missionaries to new types of work to reach people in new kinds of situations.

We see something of the challenge of tomorrow in the opportunities about us today. Our task in home missions, and our task in every church, is to try to understand, to love, to communicate and to point all people to our unchanging Lord.

THE COMMUNICATION ERA

"We must find new ways to minister to people wherever they are, whether in the 'amen corner' at church or in a tent beside a lake."

Our twentieth century missions frontiers must be seen in terms of people—people who are living a different kind of life from that of their parents and grandparents. The advances of science and technology since World War II are amazing. And they have changed the pattern of life for practically every citizen. In some ways these advances make it harder for people to get quiet enough and humble enough to hear the gospel. In other ways they have multiplied the opportunities before us for sharing the gospel.

Some senior adults can remember when telephones were few and far between, and the service was often unsatisfactory. They can remember the introduction of radio and the thrill of hearing human voices from afar. And it doesn't take a senior adult to remember when television entered our homes. The first *Early Bird* satellite, sent aloft in 1965, provided direct telephone linkage between the United States and Europe, and paved the way for telecasts from overseas and from space. Picturephones are in limited use, enabling us to see the person we are talking with across the miles. It was only a few years ago that cassette tapes, with recorders and receivers, came into wide use as a means of sharing messages and meetings. Now videotapes have provided new vehicles for teaching, training and other communication.

During the past decade we have rocketed into outer space. We have seen clear pictures from the surface of Mars, 60 million miles away. We have seen Apollo vehicles blast off and splash down. We have had ringside seats as astronauts walked in space and men conducted scientific experiments on the moon. Just three years ago we saw the pioneering *Skylab* mission overcome serious difficulties to complete its 28-day scientific journey. This was followed quickly by the 59-day mission of *Skylab II* and the 84-day mission of *Skylab III*.

Knowledge is expected to continue to double at least every 15 years. It will multiply so rapidly that agencies that gather and process information will be unable to keep up. Individuals will find it almost impossible to stay abreast outside a very narrow span.

This is indeed a time of remarkable progress in putting persons in touch with the rest of their country, their planet and their universe. It is the era of communications. These breathtaking changes have opened up enormous new opportunities and challenges for Christians who take seriously their Lord's command to bear witness to him.

Communication at Our Fingertips

There was a time when we read Buck Rogers and Flash Gordon cartoon strips and marveled. The cartoons dealt with matters far removed from us then, and today's amazing developments may seem just as far away. Nevertheless our lives are touched in a hundred ways, and our lifestyles are altered radically because of scientific advances. The communications era has touched our lives at many points. Let us look particularly at television, the computer and travel.

Television.—As early as 10 years ago there were more television sets in the United States than households. Cable television (CATV) has become so effective that some believe homes throughout the nation soon can be wired for television as they now are wired for telephone.

By the time an average American youth has completed high school he has viewed television more hours than he has spent in the schoolroom. A typical American adult views television an average of five hours a day. An advertising organization reported that the average individual has 1,600 commercial messages beamed toward him daily. Of these he consciously notices 80 and responds in some way to 12. Not all these messages come via television, but many do.

In spite of the low quality of some programming, the selective viewer can find much that is educational, wholesomely entertaining and even spiritually and morally uplifting. And television's potential for educational uses is unlimited. Some foresee the use of this medium in formal education to provide diversified and individualized programming according to the student's needs and learning rate.

Whatever the future of television may be, thoughtful Christians will see in the medium both a challenge and an opportunity. The television set now occupies much of the time once spent in conversation, reading, music and art. If the average American responds to only 12 of 1,600 messages beamed toward him in a day, it is obvious that the gospel faces stubborn competition for a hearing. We are jabbed awake to the fact that we must develop the most attractive and persuasive means we can find to reach the ears of the people who need Christ and the fellowship of the church.

The Home Mission Board began to experiment with television as a witnessing tool a few years ago. During the Crusade of the Americas in 1968-69 the Board sponsored three prime-time 30-minute specials. Four years later the Board launched a weekly half-hour program "Spring Street, USA," produced for the Board by the Southern Baptist Convention's Radio and Television Commission. The program followed a variety format beamed especially toward the unchurched.

Television undertakings are extremely expensive, and the Board initiated the effort on a financial shoestring. Cooperative Program and Annie Armstrong Easter Offering contributions provided costs, plus some funds for the purchase of station time. It is hoped that mail receipts will soon be adequate to pay for a substantial portion of the costs.

It is the Board's hope to continue an evangelistic television ministry, on an increasing number of stations and with mounting spiritual effectiveness. Financial support is the key to the Board's ability to enlarge its evangelistic ministry in these ways. In our commitment to point people to Jesus Christ it is important to use every available medium to the maximum. This is certainly true of a mission board with heavy responsibilities as an arm of the churches to reach out across the nation in Christ's name.

Hartford, Connecticut, furnished the setting for an unusual use of television in evangelizing a home missions field in 1973. Eight Southern Baptist churches in the immediate area participated. These included three Slavic, two Spanish language, one Negro, and two other English language churches. Services and witnessing conducted by the churches were augmented extensively by television and radio programs on stations in Hartford and nearby cities. A final rally, held on Sunday afternoon, attracted a full house and good response.

For years the Board has been involved in a radio ministry. At this time the Board provides human and financial resources for broadcasting the gospel in 23 languages over more than 235 stations. These broadcasts undergird the ministry of home missionaries to ethnic peoples in making friends, winning converts and forming churches. The broadcasts will continue to cross barriers of language and culture with the gospel.

The Computer.—First radio and then television put us in immediate touch with people and places hundreds of miles away. These were remarkable breakthroughs in the transmission of information. But it is the computer that has enabled us to process massive amounts of information with speed and accuracy. One of the developers of computers recently commented that there aren't enough people in the world to handle the work being done by the computers operating in the United States. Computers have become so essential to business that we now have continental and global networks of computer centers.

What does all this mean to Christians who are concerned about the spiritual stamina of their nation? Along with the computer's great benefits, there are some problems.

All of us have sensed to some degree the drawbacks of computerization. We have felt its depersonalizing effects. Our records are processed by number—though our names are there—at the bank, the gasoline company, the department store, the social security office, the university. Followers of Christ must be concerned about anything that dehumanizes persons.

But computers have opened to us a number of fresh opportunities. Working hours have been shortened. People with even modest incomes have conveniences and opportunities never dreamed of as recently as a century ago. And what lies ahead defies our ability to imagine!

Social engineering uses computers to study troubled human beings and to help these persons solve certain kinds of problems. "Predictive medicine" on a wide scale is just around the corner, through the abilities of the computer.

Travel.—The automobile's greatest development has come during the past 30 years. There are more automobiles in the United States than households, and there are thousands of two-car and three-car families. We depend on our automobiles to such an extent that traffic congestion is one of the American city's major problems; highways are crowded during vacation seasons and weekends.

The interstate superhighway has replaced the old two-lane road. Speed and congestion have brought us to the point that our death toll on the highways exceeded 50,000 annually during recent years. One of the benefits of the energy crisis has been a reduction of highway fatalities, at least for a while. But this combination of automobiles and roads has enabled vast numbers of Americans to get acquainted with people and places far removed from their home bases.

The development of the airplane has been even more fantastic. Jet planes, including the newer small jets, have put us within a few hours flying time of the rest of the nation. A flight from Atlanta to Seattle requires only four and a half hours non-stop, and within a few more hours one can reach Anchorage or Honolulu. During the past decade people who had never traveled far from their homes have flown to other continents. The airplane has enabled businesses and governments to move quickly in handling their responsibilities.

Air travel has literally revolutionized the Home Mission Board's ability to serve a nation. It took Joseph Walker nearly a month to travel from St. Louis to Marion, Alabama, 121 years ago as he assumed leadership of the young Domestic (Home) Mission Board. Today it takes only 80 minutes to fly from the Board's location in Atlanta to St. Louis. With the aid of air travel Home Mission Board staff and missionaries can give maximum field time in service, with only a minimum amount of time spent in travel.

Expanded communication has made a terrific impact on our society and our individual lives. For one thing, the awareness of what others have and are able to do has created huge appetites for more of everything. This exposure has an unsettling effect on the disadvantaged, while it makes the advantaged more difficult to please and perhaps less appreciative of the privileges they have.

On the positive side, such exposure gives promise of promoting national unity and understanding. People from all parts of the nation hear the same news commentators, view the same sports events, buy and use the same products and visit the same national parks. In the face of such sharing of impressions it will become increasingly difficult for regional differences to persist. Such interchange should contribute strongly to the elimination of regional prejudices.

And because of the international dimensions of television and travel, such exciting developments should improve international understanding, as indeed they already have done. Our growing awareness of the peoples of other lands undergirds the Christian view of the worth of all persons and of God's love for all the people of all the earth. We are living in times of amazing scientific achievement and unparalleled communications. Such an era has produced many changes in America and promises others. We must bear these changes in mind as we seek to cross barriers of every kind to share with others the love of God in Jesus Christ.

Barriers and Bridges

A 23-page magazine report on "How America is Changing" led off with the statement that "for better or worse, a different kind of U.S. is taking shape as the nation nears its 200th birthday."[3] Obvious changes which affect home missions efforts lie at the points of the increased leisure time and the high mobility of the average American, coupled with fresh challenges to spiritual and moral values.

Leisure.—In 1900 the work week in the United

States averaged 60.1 hours. This figure has declined steadily to about 35 hours today, and is expected to dip under 30 hours a week by the year 2000. To look at it another way, the average worker today has a total of 22 years more free time during his life than his grandfather had.

Commentator Eric Sevareid declared a few years ago that "the greatest challenge facing America today is the use of leisure time, and the fact that those who have the most of it know the least how to use it." It is a challenge to churches. Can the churches teach their people to use time to strengthen their faith, deepen their compassion, increase their service to others, and achieve worthy and satisfying lives?

It is estimated that 75 percent of all free time is spent at home. Surely this is a plus for the family. But this leaves 25 percent of free time for activities away from home. Free time plus affluence has enabled many families to invest in boats, lake houses, second homes and recreation vehicles.

Travel has become so much a part of the American way of life that tourism is one of the top three income sources in two thirds of the 50 states. Yellowstone and other public parks first encountered severe crowding only a few years ago. There is extensive weekend travel to nearby lakes and mountains and beaches. Visits with relatives in other localities have become routine, often on weekends. And the long-range outlook is not for less but more travel.

This situation challenges churches and missionaries to creativity. We must find ways to minister to people wherever they are, whether in "the amen corner" at church or in a tent beside a lake. A Thursday night church service might fill a need in some places. The service could even include a challenge to those headed for resort areas to live their faith there. A prayer of commitment for these short-term missionaries could be a source of strength. Churches near resort areas can look upon vast influxes of people over weekends and during holiday seasons not as a burden to be endured but as an opportunity for expanding their Christian witness.

During recent years the Home Mission Board has been involved in helping churches establish a Christian witness to visitors. It has conducted conferences and produced literature to interpret needs and find ways of meeting these needs. The Board has worked with state conventions, associations and churches in establishing resort ministries. It has commissioned missionary personnel to serve in resort settings.

Just three years ago the Home Mission Board conducted the first Southern Baptist national resort missions conference. It was attended by 175 pastors, laypersons, and missionaries from such places as Lake Tahoe, California; West Yellowstone, Montana; Grand Canyon, Arizona; and Taos, New Mexico. The agenda dealt with ways of witnessing in camping and other resort areas. It provided a resort setting in Georgia for the immediate testing of their ideas. The Board will doubtless conduct additional resort conferences as needed, such as during home missions weeks at Glorieta and Ridgecrest.

An exciting witness in resort settings is a ministry in hotels. Churches and pastors in Hawaii have conducted services in vacation-oriented hotels with outstanding responses. A decade ago home missionary Hermon S. Ray, pastor of the Waikiki Baptist Church of Honolulu and a pioneer in this ministry, led in a half-dozen worship services in hotels before noon on Sunday mornings. Assisted by volunteer church workers and his missionary wife, he would move rapidly from one 30-minute service to another, sharing the gospel warmly with visitors to the fiftieth state.

Youth groups have engaged in witnessing ministries at beaches in Florida and on ski slopes in
Colorado. They have operated coffeehouses, presented
folk music programs, shown films, offered counseling
and Bible study, and have used every means available
for person-to-person sharing of their faith in Christ.
The Board has joined with state conventions and
nearby churches and associations in sponsoring these.

Seven years ago the Board linked hands with North
Carolina Baptists in launching an extensive ministry
in resort areas such as Kitty Hawk, White Lake,
Lake Norman and Bear Den Campground. Traditional
church programs were effective, with from 100 to 600
attending Sunday School each Sunday in each of
these places. The workers also provided such special
opportunities and ministries as movies on the beach
on weeknights, an all-day Fourth of July celebration,
counseling services and midnight worship services in
a circus tent on Saturday nights.

As North Carolina missions leader, Roy J. Smith,
summarized these exciting activities, he recalled a
young woman who worked in a resort-oriented
restaurant to earn money for her college tuition. She
brought her father to the resort minister toward the
end of the season and said, "Daddy, I want you to
know this man. He and the others here are responsible
for keeping me from giving up and giving in."

In the circus tent, which served as an ice cream
parlor, students presented musical programs and gave
their testimonies. After one of the performances the
master of ceremonies was called over to the table
where a man and wife and their two teenagers were
seated. The father said, "I used to be a Christian, but I
guess I'm not any more. But I felt something here
tonight. My wife said she felt it, and our sons said
they felt it. We don't know what it is, but we don't
want to lose it. Can you tell us what this experience is

and how we might keep having this kind of feeling?" This furnished all the occasion the youth needed to talk with the family about Jesus and what he means to people in our day.

Of the many persons who visit resort areas, about 40 million are tent and vehicle campers.

In 1971 the Board initiated an unusual ministry among these people called campers on mission. Within two-and-one-half years more than 9,000 families enrolled. Each enrollee committed himself to be a Christian witness in his campground and received a COM sticker to put on his vehicle.

In the summer of 1972 the Board's Special Mission Ministries Department sponsored a campers on mission rally at Land Between the Lakes in Kentucky. Attended by 493 persons, it featured several planned activities while majoring on free time and relaxed fellowship. Mr. and Mrs. Seay Smith of Douglas, Georgia, were among those who attended. Mrs. Smith, a director of the Home Mission Board at that time, wrote glowingly of the rally. Here is part of what she put in a letter:

Before the day was over, every kind of camper you see on the highways had set up in Rushing Creek Campground. There were tents, travel trailers, pickups and mobile campers. The gear ranged from a simple Coleman stove and tent to large, homey units with all the modern equipment builders can devise. But there was one thing the same everywhere, the spirit of Christian friendliness. We have been camping for 18 years, but this is the first time we have seen and felt a complete fellowship with everyone in the campground. . . . In this age when any kind of promotion of God's Kingdom costs so much, Campers on Mission seems to be the natural and most logical means of encouraging individual witnessing at a minimum expense. Person to person witnessing through kindness and helpfulness is the basis of real evangelism. Campers on mission can be an effective and inexpensive way to witness and help laypeople overcome timidity and reserve in witnessing. . . .

To my husband and me, it was all a joy and inspiration which we will long remember. We are indeed grateful to the Home Mission Board for beginning now to plan for the future as well as the present, for these people who leave home and church to relax.

This is only a beginning, as Mrs. Smith recognized, but it opened up a way of sharing Christ with hundreds of people who were not within effective reach of a church at that time and in some cases at any time. In the years ahead, this ministry is expected to enroll many more Baptist campers and to extend into a growing number of camps.

Mobility.—More than one fourth of the American people live outside the state of their birth. Nearly half of our people moved between 1965 and 1970, and no difference is expected when the next five years' statistics are tabulated. Mobility is a distinct mark of Americans. One report stated that the average American moves 14 times in a lifetime, compared with eight by Britons and five by Japanese. The majority of persons who change residence move toward areas of higher population density—to the housing project, the dormitory or apartment, the retirement center. Even families moving to the suburbs often encounter overcrowded schools, jammed shopping centers and crowded streets and highways. Each move requires a certain amount of adjustment. Where these adjustments are not made well, it is common that crime rates rise, marriages are strained, racial and cultural clashes result, and churches are sometimes divided. Frequent moving tends to produce a sense of rootlessness. These modern nomads have no strong commitment to government or community—they do not expect to be in their present location long—and obviously most have no strong commitment to the cause of Christ as expressed in a specific place.

Because they are more difficult to reach, the temptation is for churches to put forth less effort to minister to such people than to the more permanent. In many cases there is neither time nor opportunity to develop the kind of relationship which will enable the church to minister effectively.

But there is another side. At the time of a move, people usually are responsive to spiritual approaches from their new neighbors. It is an opportune time for a fresh beginning in their spiritual and moral experience, which many realize they need. The opportunity to minister to people of different backgrounds as they move into a church's community presents another challenge. It confronts the congregation with the necessity of looking upon people as persons, regardless of their lifestyle or nationality.

In the face of this factor, what is the Home Mission Board doing? What does it propose to do?

The Board works with state conventions in starting work in diverse communities. This includes towns with a mobile population. Sometimes these projects require support from home mission funds for many years. Help is often needed to pay the pastor or other missionary worker, but a concern for people makes this investment worthwhile.

The Board sponsored a nation-wide conference on the mobile American in 1975. Out of this conference progress is expected in building bridges across the barrier of mobility. As we look beyond our Bicentennial there is no indication that mobility will decrease. It is not possible to predict with assurance what approaches will be used in home missions ministries to the moving multitudes. But this should not reduce our desire or efforts to win such people to Christ.

Values.—As we celebrate our two-hundredth anniversary it may be that we are more truly a national society than ever before, rather than a grouping of regional units. This is one of the reasons that we recently have become more aware of group needs— the needs of blacks, Indians, Chicanos, youth, the elderly, women. We are consciously a pluralistic nation. America has made room for persons of different races, subcultures, viewpoints and religions. On the surface we are a religious people. A higher percentage of Americans say they are members of churches than in any other Western country. In church attendance, America ranks high, possibly at the top. Our coins and currency bear the motto, "In God We Trust." But in the midst of these outward signs of religion, one of our serious problems is a generally weak commitment to Christ and the church.

Professor Will Herberg spoke of what he called civil religion in an interview on the future of religion in the United States. He said, "Almost nowhere else will you find the national life religionized—where national culture and religion become intermingled into a kind of civil religion." He defined this civil religion as "an organic structure of ideas, ideals, values, and beliefs that constitute a faith common to Americans as Americans, and is genuinely operative in their lives; a faith that markedly influences, and is influenced by, their professed religions."[4]

Whether we agree with Dr. Herberg's appraisals or not, they merit our consideration. His analysis must impress Christians of the great need to hold firmly to our conviction that Jesus Christ is Lord. Our objective must be clear. We are not encouraging people to be religious; we are inviting them to join us in following Christ as the only Lord and Savior.

Another serious challenge to Christian values

comes by way of the prosperity that has accompanied recent scientific advances. We are highly favored materially. The forecast is that by 1985 three fourths of all American families will have incomes in excess of $15,000 per year. This compares with slightly more than one third of our families now in this bracket.

This is a bright prospect. We are a privileged people. But it is time to see material things for what they are, and not allow financial concerns to swallow us up. It is a time to recognize that these technological advantages are not ours to use for ourselves alone. They are ours to share.

At a time in national life when a spiritual and moral rebirth is urgently needed, we must undergird our churches and their missionary outreach as never before. More than 80 million persons in our nation are not members of any religious body, and the number increases each year. How many millions of people do not know Christ, only God knows.

Recent scientific advances have resulted in changing lifestyles of practically every American. Television, the computer and travel have provided more leisure time and made us more mobile than ever before. They have also contributed to a secular viewpoint that seriously challenges traditional spiritual and moral values.

This is a time, therefore, that calls for vigorous Christian witness and ministry and for genuine Christian compassion and understanding. We have the resources to mount a more extensive and more fruitful home missions effort than ever before. Liberal support through the Cooperative Program and the annual Annie Armstrong Easter Offering are indispensable. Personal involvement and sincere prayer are fundamental ingredients as we serve Christ in the challenging years ahead.

SPOTLIGHT ON PERSONS

"Through the Home Mission Board, every church and Christian can touch thousands of persons and hundreds of places beyond their reach."

The story of 75-year-old Flora Smith could be duplicated a thousand times with only a change in name and address. Home missionary Carl Holden met this woman through the Greater Worcester (Massachusetts) Baptist Ministries, directed for many years by missionary Bob Tremaine.

Flora Smith was one of 65 elderly apartment residents who received food monthly through a surplus food delivery program. The government provided the food, and the church delivered it. As the missionary delivered food to Miss Smith's high-rise apartment he tried to help her both physically and spiritually. He became aware that Miss Smith could read very little and could write only her name. He was able to provide an instructor-friend from church members, and Miss Smith began the long-delayed path to literacy and a fuller life at her advanced age.

It has been a decade since the Home Mission Board adopted a set of long-range plans introduced by a dozen important quidelines. One guideline says: "The interest of the Home Mission Board shall be in each person because of his intrinsic worth apart from incidental identification as to race, language, economics, nationality or religion."

Miss Smith—elderly, illiterate, lonely—was one of those persons in whom home missions workers were interested because she was a person. She was loved and served by missionaries and lay workers who cared enough to help the elderly and the young, both families and individuals.

This is where the spotlight is today and must be in the future. Through the Home Mission Board, every church and every Christian can touch thousands of persons and hundreds of places beyond their immediate reach. Ministries to material need bear witness to Christ and his love for all persons. Often such ministries open tightly closed doors for helping a person to find Christ, and through him to find new hope and dignity, new purpose and power.

The Elderly

Within the next 10 years the number of Americans over 65 years of age will exceed 25 million, a gain of one fourth in just 15 years. Many of these will be taking care of themselves and will have their own home or apartment. Others will live in retirement facilities. Some will be confined to nursing homes. More adults than ever, thanks to Social Security and other retirement plans, will be able to take care of their financial needs on a reasonable standard of living.

But many elderly people have serious financial problems. Six million persons over 65 are reported to be living in poverty. More than one third of these live alone. Margaret H. Bacon, in an article titled "Why the Old Are Getting Mad," called the isolated, elderly poor "the most forgotten group in America." She noted that there are federal and state programs which make provision for such persons, but many elderly men and women do not take advantage of them because of shyness or pride or confusion. These deprived people must be a concern of Christian people. They must be a concern of home missionaries as they minister to all people.

As we peer into the future, home missions will be sensitive to the growing number of elderly people. Many missionaries whose post of service is in the inner cities will minister to hundreds of such persons. Various hospital chaplains, who relate to the denomination through the Home Mission Board, serve large numbers of elderly people.

It is not likely the Board will appoint missionaries to major on work with the aging. Instead every missionary will be alert to minister to people, whether aging or youthful, within the setting of his assignment. The Board will continue to work with Woman's Missionary Union and Brotherhood in encouraging mission action projects directed toward the elderly.

Sun City, Arizona, is one of several retirement communities scattered about the nation. With more than 30,000 retired or semi-retired residents today, it expects a population of 80,000 by 1990. Four years ago the First Baptist Church of Sun City was organized with nearly 100 members. It had been a mission of the First Southern Baptist Church of Phoenix for the previous six years. The Home Mission Board helped for a time with a pastor's salary supplement and later with a $35,000 loan to help finance the church's first building, a chapel seating 200 people.

Not only has the church moved quickly to self-support but its members are involved in a variety of mission actions. During a recent year the members provided financial assistance at two nearby missions and served as volunteer helpers in the Baptist Center in Phoenix. They conducted Sunday afternoon services at the resident hotel which houses persons who are unable to live alone or prepare their own meals. Pastor Virt spoke of the vast potential in these capable people, and added that "many express their appreciation to God for the fact he is using them as much as or more than at any time in their lives."

One of the brightest aspects of the nationwide picture is the fact that most post-65 people are in good health physically, mentally and spiritually. They constitute a giant reservoir of potential mission workers which the Board intends to tap increasingly. A year or a summer or a month working beside a missionary on a needy field would be a joyous experience for thousands of senior adults. It would greatly strengthen the Christian witness in such places.

The Young

Those who are concerned about persons must be concerned about the family. Both optimists and pessimists about the family's future recognize that today's family faces formidable difficulties. Extensive travel is required of many men and women, taking them away from the family for varying periods of time. The divorce rate continues high—about one out of every four marriages. The pressures and tempo of urbanized life greatly limit the opportunities many families have to be together in a satisfying manner. High mobility and accompanying rootlessness take their toll.

Youth appear to be hit hardest by unstable family life. Without loving, firm and consistent guidance at home, they drift into aimlessness, emptiness and substitutes for the real thing. Some turn to drugs or alcohol, and find themselves held captive. Some turn to the mystical—Zen Buddhism, Krishna consciousness, witchcraft or astrology and find themselves unsatisfied. Some turn to illicit sex and find disappointment rather than fulfillment.

Home missionaries have many opportunities to assist youth with just such problems. During his service as a US-2er Robin Rogers described his opportunity like this:

My world is 15 minutes from New York City in a middle-class residential area complete with shopping centers and supermarkets. A world not very different from your own.

In my world 95 percent of all high school students have at some time used drugs. Most everyone smokes, curses, shoplifts and plays with sex. Over 30 percent of the parents are divorced or separated, and almost half of the adult population are having affairs.

My world is Jane, who has five times attempted suicide, had a miscarriage, and lived for two years in a reform school. Jane is 15, addicted to barbiturates, and hated by her mother.

My world is 50 elderly people—very tired, very lonely, very afraid.

Dave's world is the confused, terrifying world of ups and downs, speed and freakouts. Bill's world is Harlem, the Mafia, Sing Sing and the hard, lonely life of an alcoholic. Their world is my world; a world not very different from your own.

In the middle-class suburbs I try to lead a church to involve itself in weekday ministries.

In this hypocritical, materialistic, amoral society, I try to live a life of values, a life of meaning, a life of depth.

With Jane I try to share a love of compassion instead of sex, a life of works instead of words.

With my elderly friends I try to share my hope, my destiny, myself.

Into Dave's and Bill's dark medicated world of escape I try to show that Christ is light and in him there is strength to face life and live it.

We grieve over even one young person who places a heavy mortgage on his adult life by a sordid youth, but we can find encouragement in the thousands of young people who do have ideals, character, faith and purpose. We rejoice over the thousands of high school youth who have gotten involved in summer mission activities and in new evangelistic approaches. We rejoice over college youth—more than 1,000 strong annually for the past few years—who have invested 10 weeks of their lives as student summer missionaries. We rejoice over college students serving at other times of the year for brief periods. Their service is outstanding and what happens to the youth is significant.

Home missions will continue to count on young people for short-term ministries throughout the year. And home missions will continue to reach out loving hands to youth in trouble, and their families, through compassionate missionaries and ministries.

The Disadvantaged

Though the United States reaches its two-hundredth birthday as an affluent nation, millions of her people have little share in its prosperity.

Most towns have slums. Here are poor people, of whatever race, often poorly housed, unemployed or underemployed, and defeated in spirit. Some are victims of their own moral and spiritual failure. Some are victims of forces beyond their control. Some are victims of crippling physical and mental handicaps. Some are poorly qualified for the kinds of jobs available in today's world. Their offspring grow up in such a depressing atmosphere that some are trapped by a sense of hopelessness even from childhood. It is not surprising that too often crime, vice, alcohol and drugs gain the upper hand on integrity and faith.

The 2 million migrant farm workers of our nation

face critical problems. Living in their home communities only a few months a year, they suffer handicaps and indignities.

It was a special joy to meet Fermin Flores when he came for missionary orientation about three years ago. A teacher on the faculty of the Mexican Baptist Bible Institute in Texas, Flores had grown up in a migrant family. Determined to get an education he finished high school at 22, then went on to the University of Corpus Christi, Texas, and Southwestern Baptist Theological Seminary. Fermin Flores' pilgrimage from migrant family to a commitment to Christ and a missionary calling speaks of what God can do for a person who will give him a chance.

For many years Southern Baptists have been actively involved in ministries to migrants. For a time the Home Mission Board employed missionaries who moved with the migrants and shared the gospel with them in every way possible. The present plan calls for a limited number of missionaries who work primarily with churches and associations. They move ahead of the migrant workers and help churches and associations to plan and provide needed ministries for these short-term residents of their areas.

In every community are people whose lives are dull, monotonous, lonely and purposeless. The most transforming message in the world is the truth that under God every person is of worth. Every person has possibilities and responsibilities. God loves the poorest, the weakest, the most defeated, the most unpromising person in the world.

Many of these disadvantaged people live in the inner city where change and decay are the order of the day. It was only a few years ago that the Montgomery (Alabama) Baptist Association initiated a program of Christian social ministries beamed toward such people. The Home Mission Board joined the Alabama

Baptist State Convention and the association in employing home missionary Gladys Farmer as ministries director. From the Baptist Center Building—a former Jewish synagogue—Baptists soon reached into 10 areas of Montgomery and touched persons of eight nationalities in the name of Jesus. Led by Miss Farmer, the churches responded so beautifully that within two years almost 500 regular volunteer workers, plus 300 rotating volunteers, vere involved in weekday ministries. They served hot meals to shut-ins once a week. They provided transportation, food and clothing for those in need of such help. They provided classes in sewing, nutrition, good grooming, typing, crafts and literacy. They operated a coffeehouse for youth activities.

Miss Farmer described her task as seeking to meet needs in three categories: physical, emotional and spiritual. Physical needs were met with clothing, food, housing and jobs. Emotional needs were met through understanding, acceptance and encouragement. Spiritual needs were met through the invitation to hope and salvation through Jesus Christ. Eighty-seven persons professed commitment to Christ during the first full year of this effort.

What has happened in Montgomery is happening in a hundred other cities across the nation as Southern Baptists minister to persons in special need. During this decade missionaries have reported from 3,100 to 4,500 professions of faith in Christ each year through Christian social ministries. Whatever changes the future may bring, persons will continue to need the love and encouragement of Christian people.

Expansion is the word for the future in such ministries: expansion into more and more cities in states where our work is well established; expansion in states where Southern Baptist work is still new and where our base for service is enlarging.

Those in Unusual Circumstances

One of my memorable experiences comes from a weekend spiritual retreat in a federal prison. On the invitation of a chaplain, Southern Baptist Austin L. Ingram, I brought the messages each evening and Sunday morning. I shared with the chaplain in counseling with groups and individuals. It was a blessing to see the favorable response of many.

This is what the chaplaincy is all about. It is a pastoral ministry for persons in unusual circumstances. At mid-1974, 899 Southern Baptist chaplains were ministering through all types of service, 796 serving full-time and 103 part-time. About 500 of these served in various branches of the military and almost 300 in the hospital chaplaincy. Institutional chaplains numbered more than 100 and those in industrial chaplaincy, the newest of these areas, came to 26.

Though these workers normally are employed by a government agency or private employer, they are missionaries to thousands of people who almost certainly would not be reached except for the efforts of these competent and dedicated persons.

The need for volunteer chaplaincy programs, conducted by an association or even by a single church, is pressing. Hundreds of hospitals and institutions do not have staff chaplains and will not find it feasible to do so. Hospitals, nursing homes, institutions for the care of persons with special problems, and jails furnish the churches with prime opportunities to minister to people in great need.

Minority Peoples

Concern for persons moves the spotlight to minority peoples. At least 120 ethnic groups, using 85 languages and accounting for almost half of the national population, are a part of the United States.

In the 1970 census 70 million persons identified themselves as foreign born or with a foreign-born parent, in addition to more than 23 million black Americans. More Spanish-speaking people live in Los Angeles than in any other city in North America except Mexico City. More Polish people live in Chicago than in any other city in the world except Warsaw. The Cuban population in Miami is surpassed only by Havana's. The Puerto Rican population in New York City is second only to San Juan's. The number of blacks in New York City is larger than in any city in the world except Ibadan and Lagos, Nigeria.

Thousands of these people are Southern Baptists. They hold membership in hundreds of churches. The majority belong to some 2,000 Southern Baptist churches and missions which are composed largely of their own ethnic group. More than 1,000 of these churches and missions are Spanish-language congregations, more than 400 are Indian, in excess of 250 are European, and over 50 are Oriental. Close to 200 black churches cooperate with the Southern Baptist Convention and 800 or more other Southern Baptist Convention churches have black members.

The Negro.—Negroes constitute the largest racial minority group in the nation. If there was ever a time when Southern Baptists could ignore their relationship to blacks, that time is past. Court decisions, civil rights legislation, and demonstrations of the past 22 years have called the American people forcibly to a clear change of course. We have experienced a revolution in two decades, and much remains to be done by both blacks and whites.

Unlike the members of all other minority groups in this country, Negroes are predominantly Protestant Christians. Of those belonging to any church, the overwhelming majority are Baptists. Black Baptist churches work together through one or another of three National Baptist Conventions which have a combined membership of over 8 million people.

In the Home Mission Board's early decades it sought to carry the gospel to blacks (and Indians) as well as whites. God blessed these efforts. The present plan calls for working together so both Southern Baptists and National Baptists strengthen their witness. The Board has joined with 15 SBC-related state conventions in employing a state director of cooperative ministries with National Baptists. These men, such as long-time workers Loren Belt of Missouri and Tom L. Pfeifer of Louisiana, have built bridges of Christian cooperation and understanding between National and Southern Baptists.

Missionaries and budgets of the Board relate to black people in many ways and through various ministries. For example, church extension guidance and funds are available to Southern Baptist churches regardless of race, such as assistance on pastor's salary for the all-black Antioch Baptist Church of Connecticut. This congregation was sponsored by the First Baptist Church of East Hartford, Connecticut, a Southern Baptist church. Several missionaries, such as Mildred Streeter at Carver Center, New Orleans, and Bobbie Jean Murphy at Johenning Center in the nation's capital, minister to large numbers of Negro youth and adults.

Negroes account for approximately one in nine persons in the United States today. This ratio is expected to become one in seven by 1985, with a total Negro population of 34 million. Our relationships with blacks present one of the clearest challenges before Southern Baptists as a denomination. They offer one of our outstanding opportunities for advancing the cause of Christ and healing divisions within our nation.

Other minority peoples.—The growing number of ethnics is one of the striking changes in our nation. During the 1960s growth patterns shifted away from European to Asian and South and Central American groups. There was little immigration from Europe, and many residents of European descent moved into the mainstream of American life. On the other hand, Orientals increased more than 50 percent during the 1960s to about 1.5 million persons.

The number who use Spanish as their primary language, though they may speak English, reached 6.2 million in 1970. While the white population was climbing 12 percent between the 1960 and 1970 censuses, Negroes increased 20 percent and Indians 51 percent.

Color and race will become less and less significant to the American people if present trends continue. There will continue to be recognition of differences of language, culture and color, but with the awareness that differences do not classify one as inferior and another as superior. This is something of the genius of the United States, with "government of the people, by the people, and for the people"—all the people. This lies at the heart of Christianity, with love for God and love for persons at the center of its lifestyle.

The Nineteenth Avenue Baptist Church of San Francisco, for many years a home missions congregation, showed this spirit beautifully a few years ago when they shared their building with a Chinese congregation. The groups used some of the same facilities, with a staggered schedule of services. The Chinese congregation grew to such size and strength that the Anglo group took the initiative in proposing joint ownership of the property.

In the meantime they had opened their facilities to a third group, a Japanese mission congregation. Two churches and a mission—three congregations of differing ethnic identities—thereby used the same property. These servants of God were exercising wise stewardship in an area of skyrocketing real estate prices and shortage of available facilities for church use. More importantly, they were demonstrating Christian love beautifully across ethnic lines.

Language-group churches often become bases for missionary outreach. Only a few years ago the First Chinese Baptist Church of Los Angeles established a mission in Sacramento. Laypersons traveled the 800-mile round trip weekly to work in the mission. The First Papago (Indian) Baptist Church in Sells, Arizona, operated a home for foster children, child care and kindergarten facilities at the invitation of the Bureau of Indian Affairs, and at no expense to the Home Mission Board.

The increasing aggressiveness of both Indians and Spanish language people is expected to continue. The confrontation of the American Indian Movement (AIM) and the United States government at Wounded Knee, South Dakota, pointed up the need for Southern Baptists to rethink missions to American Indians.

It is obvious now that in working with any minority group, leadership must increasingly be placed with members of that particular group. This is not a new insight with the Board, but one which recent events have underlined dramatically. Three years ago the Board appointed an Indian as coordinator of home mission work with Indians. B. Frank Belvin, long-time home missionary and a highly qualified man, was appointed to this work only a few months after the Wounded Knee experience.

For the past five years a Mexican-American, Oscar Romo, has served as leader of the Home Mission Board's language missions program. Another Mexican-American, Daniel Sanchez, is a member of the staff, along with an Indian-American, David Benham.

A black American, Emmanuel L. McCall, became director of the Department of Cooperative Ministries with National Baptists in 1975, joined by Edward L. Wheeler, also a black American. The list of home missionaries reveals that many of our workers are members of the ethnic group which they serve. You will see such names as Garcia, Rodriguez, Berkuta, Pancewicz, Wong and Kondo.

Almost half of Southern Baptists' home missionaries are language missionaries, serving with some 35 ethnic groups. This work will continue to have a high priority in home missions, but the number of language missionaries might decline.

If this happens it will be for two reasons: First, an increasing number of language congregations will assume responsibility for the support of their work; second, language missionaries will usually perform a catalytic type ministry rather than serve a single congregation. They will give their time to train pastoral and lay leaders needed in the mission congregation. They will give their time to train pastoral and lay leaders needed in the mission congregations. A slight decrease in the number of language missionaries has already occurred for these reasons.

Sometimes a question is raised as to the appropriateness of Southern Baptists' providing help to minority groups. It is asked whether this may not support segregation. The Board's viewpoint is that our task as Christians is to reach people for Christ in whatever honorable manner they can be touched. It is the Board's experience that many ethnics will not be reached unless at least the initial approach is made through a congenial culture group. In addition to helping language congregations, the Board encourages Anglo churches to open their doors and ministries to all people. The Board assists wherever its help is requested and resources permit. Numerous Southern Baptist churches have members from non-Anglo-Saxon backgrounds. Fully 1,500 churches conduct specific ministries to such persons, including ministries to deaf and Internationals. This number of churches will continue to grow.

Deaf.—The Board's concern for deaf people is expressed through its language missions program. About 250,000 deaf people live in the United States. The Board's small staff of missionaries to the deaf, fewer than 35, majors on enlisting churches and training workers in volunteer ministries.

Several of these missionaries, such as David and Patricia Richardson in Alabama and John and Ina Cooper in the Great Lakes area, serve an entire state or region. Clifford and Ruth Ann Bruffey minister at Gallaudet College for the deaf in the District of Columbia, and Carter and Wanda Bearden serve as consultants throughout the nation.

Internationals.—The people whom Southern Baptists call "Internationals" and whom the United States Immigration and Naturalization Service calls "nonimmigrants" constitute a challenge and opportunity for American Christians. The total number of these people has exceeded 4 million annually during recent years. The majority come to the U.S. on pleasure trips. Diplomatic representatives, together with office staffs and family members, number more than 65,000. Students account for more than 160,000 each year, and many of these remain four years or longer.

Some come from lands which are closed to Christian missionary efforts. Some come from nations which are predominantly Moslem, Jewish, Buddhist or communist. Some of these Internationals, therefore, present our best and possibly our only opportunity to enter their homelands with the gospel. If our quality of life and our Christian witness can be used by God to lead even 1 percent of these influential people to follow Christ, they will constitute an impressive force for the Christian gospel in their homelands.

Business visitors offer an additional opportunity. They will be in the States from a few days to months, and in some cases for long-term residence. The United States' development of trade and business agreements with China and Russia, and the increasing business involvement of Japan, along with other international understandings, opens the prospect of massive growth of multinational companies.

One business writer has forecast that such growth could well bring from 20 to 50 times more business persons to the United States in the decade ahead than in the years just past. This would escalate the number of business visitors to the 1 million to 3 million range each year. We must devise denominational strategies and provide helps for Christian business persons in sharing of their faith with their associates from overseas. The Brotherhood Commission and the Home Mission Board doubtless will give serious attention to this emerging opportunity, and hundreds of laypeople will grasp this unusual privilege of service.

There are 118 embassies and three legations in the United States, a total of 121 diplomatic corps. The embassies in our nation's capital maintain staffs totaling at least 3,000 employees. Many of these are married and bring their families with them. Their children, including those from communist countries, usually attend our public schools and universities.

The need and challenge in Washington is so great that five years ago the Board appointed Minor and Mary Davidson as missionaries to work with the District of Columbia Baptist Convention and nearby churches in developing strategies for Christian witness among these influential people. Two years ago Elias Golonka, a former Home Mission Board staff member, and his wife, Nancy, were given a similar assignment in the challenging international field in New York City.

Students with inquiring minds offer an exciting opportunity. Denominational leadership for the work with international students is an assignment of the National Student Ministries Program of the Sunday School Board. Campus ministers throughout the nation give attention to the strategic opportunity in this area. Large numbers of home missionaries find international students in their respective fields and work with churches in trying to reach them for Christ. This is particularly true of certain language congregations, such as the Berendo Street Baptist Church in Los Angeles, where Don and Esther Kim, natives of Korea, serve. This congregation was an object of Home Mission Board support for several years, and is now a strong, self-supporting, truly international church.

*   *   *

Home missions includes special efforts to reach such groups as the elderly, the young, the disadvantaged, persons in unusual circumstances and minority peoples. It is likely that in the years before us fresh channels of sharing the gospel with other groups will be discovered.

The basic concern for persons must include people in all walks of life. It must include the professional and the laborer, the prosperous and the poor, the sophisticated and the unlearned, the healthy and the sick, the free and the imprisoned, the civilian and the military, the Anglo and the ethnic. Through needed new churches and evangelistic efforts and through every home missions program, the unchanging objective will continue to be to lead persons to follow Jesus Christ as Lord and Savior. The spotlight is on all persons, with their strengths and their weaknesses, their righteousness and their sins.

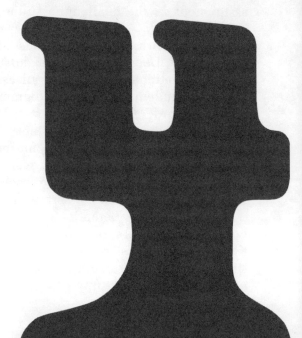

TECHNIQUES
IN
TRANSITION

"The attitude of the Home Mission Board has been one of firmness and flexibility—firmness of purpose and flexibility of method."

Persons who have attended recent home missions conferences have heard about new and effective techniques in home missions. They have seen some of the new equipment used to cross barriers with the gospel.

A few summers ago, West Virginia missionaries had a bookmobile on display at Ridgecrest Baptist Conference Center. It was being operated by Southern Baptists of the Upper Ohio Valley Area in West Virginia. The side panels of the vehicle identified it in large, clear lettering:

GOOD NEWS
BOOKMOBILE
Sponsored By
SOUTHERN BAPTISTS
BOOKS LOANED *FREE* TO ALL AGES.

The six Southern Baptist churches in this nine-county field faced the question of how they could minister effectively to the 300,000 people in their area. They came up with a unique approach—a bookmobile. The Home Mission Board approved the proposal as a pilot missions project, in cooperation with the West Virginia Baptist convention and the association. The Board purchased the 12-foot step-up van and paid for the shelving inside the van. It also employed a US-2 couple, Howard and Martha Beam, to use the vehicle in a traveling library ministry. The Church Library Department of the Sunday School Board designed the inside plan of the van and provided training for workers. The upper Ohio Valley Baptist Association provided help in book processing and in training more workers. The American Bible Society provided large-print Bibles and New Testaments. Television and radio stations and newspapers publicized the service throughout the area. Church announcements, posters and handbills provided current information about the bookmobile's schedule. During the first year, an average of more than 80 books a week were checked out. By the end of the year the library totaled over 2,300 books, largely religious but some of general interest. More than 4,000 persons visited the vehicle during this time. The route of 1,100 miles a month called for travel Tuesdays through Fridays in the afternoons and early evenings. Its weekly stops included schools, grocery stores, community buildings, missions and church buildings. It attracted hosts of unchurched people in a state in which only about 30 percent of the population belongs to any church.

Then there is the Chapel on Wheels, an outreach ministry of the Kern County Southern Baptist Association, with churches in and near Bakersfield, California. The chapel is a city bus which has been converted into a teaching and worship facility. This is a cooperative project which includes the California state convention and the Home Mission Board along with the association. Missionaries Meredith and Pearl Wyatt share teaching responsibilities. They move from place to place to organize and conduct Bible classes, play recorded music, show films and filmstrips, porvide library services and conduct worship services.

The Wyatts have established ministries wherever there were people in need and where attention could be gained. They have worked with youth near their schools. They have conducted activities for persons of all ages in homes, at shopping centers, on campgrounds, in parks and at the county fairground. They have met an outstanding response.

One of the highlights of the first year's work was

the children's Bible clubs, held once a week after school. Including fun things as well as Bible teaching, these clubs attracted an average of 205 a week from October through June. Twenty-seven professed faith in Christ.

Bible classes were established for students of two elementary and one junior high school, in agreement with school officials and with parental permission. More than 200 enrolled in these weekly classes. Audiovisual aids were used extensively.

These approaches were used in small towns and in the city. They were used in both high-income and low-income communities. They were used among both blacks and whites.

During the summer the bus provided space for mission Vacation Bible Schools and day camps.

A variety of one-shot activities included choir and film programs at shopping centers, programs at resort areas, and a nine-day stand at the county fair. The fairground situation afforded the associational Woman's Missionary Union an opportunity to both provide hospitality and to offer Christian witness.

In both the Upper Ohio Valley Association and the Kern County Association, churches maintained and promoted the traditional ways of teaching, training, worship and witness. And God blessed. In addition they found exciting new ways of going out to people who were not attending any church and who were not following Christ.

Compassion for people and commitment to the great commission of our Lord are essential. It is this which has propelled home missionaries, and concerned pastors and laypersons as well, out where Christless people are. Such Christians have found ways of carrying the knowledge of Christ across the barriers that separate people from the Lord and his church.

We have become familiar with other fruitful new approaches. Some of these are:

- Bible study groups in homes, especially involving young adults;
- coffeehouses, appealing primarily to youth and often to young people with serious spiritual and moral needs;
- community ministries, ranging from day care to well-baby clinics, from drug rehabilitation to tutoring help;
- varied ministries with people in apartment complexes, mobile home parks and resort areas.

People's needs remain unchanged, and the gospel remains unchanged. But methods of attracting people to the gospel have *had* to change. The power is in the gospel, not in methods. In this spirit, home missionaries are urged to use every method which their imaginations can conjure up to fulfill their mission. We throw out the same challenge to churches and individual Christians across the Convention.

What changed methods the future will call for, only God knows. But we human beings can be sure that changes will continue—and will even speed up. The effective methods of today will have to be revised constantly or scrapped in favor of better ways of carrying the gospel to persons without Christ.

Closing the Bypass

In other years we planned church programs to relate to people of the neighborhood around the church building. In a high percentage of families today, however, the people have other ties which are closer than those with their neighbors. The young often find their closest friends at school, rather than in the neighborhood. Men and women often find their most meaningful friendships among those with whom they work. Others find their warmest ties with their golfing or fishing associates, or their fellow members in civic or garden clubs.

Today's people live in several worlds at once—the world of daily work, the world of recreation, the world of neighborhood. The widespread loss of a sense of neighborhood has left a vacuum which presents an outstanding opportunity for churches. God placed within man a desire for comradeship. We are not at our best when we stand alone. We need others. The Christian fellowship is equipped to respond well to this need.

This weakening of neighborhood ties requires that we find additional avenues for sharing our Christian faith. Some past home missions efforts point in this direction. This is particularly true of approaches made to men and women through the channels of their daily work. Sometimes the vocation is such that Christians might easily pass these people by on the other side, as the priest and Levite did in Jesus' parable of the good Samaritan.

One such ministry is that carried on by missionaries James and Janice Reid on "The Strip" in Las Vegas, Nevada. Begun six years ago under Home Mission Board sponsorship, this is largely a nighttime or early morning ministry. The Reids provide Bible classes, discussion goups, personal counseling and worship opportunities for persons employed by the hotels, motels and casinos. Without condoning the lifestyle or the work of these men and women, the Reids represent Baptists in expressing the love of Christ for all persons.

Another group which Christian people usually pass by is racetrack employees. These people became a high priority concern of some Baptists in Florida a few years ago. Horace "Salty" Roberts, a converted race track employee, and Ernest R. Campbell, pastor of the First Baptist Church of Hialeah, Florida, helped form the Race Track Chaplaincy of America, a non-profit corporation. By the middle of 1974 it had appointed six full-time chaplains to minister at six different tracks. The first of these permanent full-time chaplains was a former Southern Baptist pastor in Hialeah, Cliff Hoolsema.

He described these people as "real losers," living and working at the track, often friendless, and many times facing severe drug, alcohol and family problems. "My aim," he said, "is to bring the peace and contentment of knowing Christ to these people." The Home Mission Board has demonstrated its sympathy with the effort and keeps in touch through its Division of Chaplaincy.

Still another group which has become an increasing concern to many Southern Baptists is foreign seamen who come into American ports. They reach the staggering total of over 2 million a year, coming on approximately 75,000 vessels.

Two missionary couples give direction to such a ministry along with their other services to language peoples and Internationals. Charles and Betty Lawhon direct this ministry for the Jacksonville (Florida) Baptist Association, and missionaries Ivan and Louracia de Souza are heavily involved in similar work for the Mobile (Alabama) Baptist Association. One of de Souza's reports, covering slightly more than a month, stated that more than 800 seamen had attended services and participated in recreational activities, and 15 seamen had made decisions for Christ. In Jacksonville, Lawhon reported visiting 97 ships from 40 different countries, and an excellent response. Both these programs maintain a center which is staffed by volunteer workers from churches.

The Gulf Stream Baptist Association (Florida), with offices in Fort Lauderdale, employed a full-time chaplain, Howard Botts, at Port Everglades four years ago. The association has built a center for its ministries to seamen. The Home Mission Board does not contribute toward the chaplain's salary, but has provided small grants in support of the work. One of the inspiring expressions of this ministry is the involvement of local churches.

Members of the First Baptist Church of Lacey, Washington, ministering to seamen at the port of Tacoma, and members of the Highland Avenue Baptist Church, Jamaica, New York, serving at the Brooklyn docks, are outstanding examples of ministries carried on by volunteers.

The oldest of the now active Baptist programs is the New Orleans Baptist Seamen's Service, Inc., directed by John P. Vandercook. Established in the early 1960s, this work is not officially related to any mission board. All of its directors, however, are Baptists. The Home Mission Board assists financially.

Director Vandercook spoke for all concerned about seamen when he wrote: "Seamen are often overlooked and forgotten (until we miss their services in supplying our needs from other countries of the world). Spiritually they are forgotten people. Often those who desire to do so cannot attend church because of work or sailing schedule."

He quoted a German captain who said, "I have sailed for 47 years and you are the first to ever visit my ship to share Christmas singing with us." A Korean seaman told a group of Baptist Young Women who had conducted a worship service on his ship, "You are the first Christians to visit our ship and tell us about Jesus."

The Home Mission Board will almost certainly become more involved in ministries to seamen. It will go beyond the occasional financial grant and the employment of missionaries who give only part of their time to this service. The Board will provide a correlating ministry and a conference ministry, which will enable workers at the various ports to communicate with one another more effectively. It will also help in linking this ministry to our Foreign Mission Board and seaport ministries around the world.

Still other groups will become objects of compassion and assistance through home missions programs. It may be that specific ministries directed toward the blind and other handicapped persons will be established. Missionaries and churches will doubtless be encouraged to find ways of ministering more effectively to recently divorced or widowed persons. Challenging opportunities of ministries to opinion-makers across the nation are awaiting some group bold enough to move in this direction.

We must find ways of reaching such people as television script-writers and entertainers, artists and scientists, government and education officials, and professional and business leaders who are not committed Christians. Such a ministry would have to be developed by personal contacts, on a one-to-one basis. It would call for specialized missionaries with unusual abilities to relate to such influential persons in the name of Christ. This may well become one of the new and highly rewarding aspects of Southern Baptist home missions in the decades ahead.

While we have all too often bypassed disadvantaged persons, we have more frequently bypassed persons whose character and spiritual outlook influence the character of a city, a state or the nation. All bypasses must be closed! New ways of influencing such people for Christ must be opened.

An Ounce of Prevention

Another expected change in approach lies at getting at the causes of problems. Home missions has characteristically expressed compassion for the suffering, the mistreated, the poor. We have been willing to give to people in need, but have not always tried to help them get on their feet and support themselves. An old proverb goes something like this: "Give a man a fish and you feed him once. Teach a man to fish, and you help him feed himself a lifetime."

It is true that everything we do to help persons find Christ as the controlling center of their lives is preventive. When a person truly becomes a Christian he discovers a new life. He finds a new self-respect, a new motivation, a new purpose in life. He learns that however poor or humble he or his family may be, he is worth something in the sight of God: God loves him. Southern Baptists have been active in evangelism. This is the supreme preventive of broken hopes and broken homes and broken hearts. This commitment we must maintain!

Nevertheless, for many persons, life has gone hard. There are the poorly educated and the unemployable and the badly housed. Some have not gotten equal education and employment and housing opportunities because of race or sex or physical handicap. There are the hostile and the criminal, the drug addict and the alcoholic, the chronically ill and the bereaved.

In the name of Christ we must help the helpless in whatever ways open to us. But we must also find means of curing the causes of such unfortunate situations, whenever the cause can be controlled by man.

In home missions we are already at work on some of these causes. In rescue mission work, a bath, a meal, a bed and a worship service are no longer considered enough. Fresh attention has been given to counseling with each person, individually if possible. With patient and wise guidance in an atmosphere of

Christian love, many persons make a start toward a satisfying way of life.

About two decades ago the Board began a ministry to juvenile delinquents and broken homes. Later it renamed this work juvenile rehabilitation. It became apparent, however, that troubled youth usually came from troubled homes. This led both missionaries and volunteer workers to try to strengthen the family. This work is now called youth and family services.

Literacy missions was born of the same awareness of need. Sensing the great problems of adults who cannot read, the Board employed a specialist to train volunteer workers to teach non-readers. Scores of Woman's Missionary Union and Brotherhood mission action groups as well as missionaries have gotten involved in this work. They have taught thousands of persons to read and speak the English language. Such services have opened many doors for the personal sharing of Christ.

R.C. Johnson Sr., after years of fruitful juvenile rehabilitation work in Georgia, retired and moved to Statesville, N.C.—but couldn't stay retired. There he found youth who needed help, and he responded. He was the prime mover in getting a juvenile court established and then worked with the court in providing help for troubled youth. Serving as director of youth and family services for the South Yadkin Baptist Association, he discovered that most of these children had a reading handicap. He enlisted more than 40 volunteer tutors from churches and schools, and trained them with the aid of a literacy specialist. Youngsters with school problems were assigned to a tutor near them.

In six months the number of youth coming to the court was cut in half. Schoolteachers of children in the program reported a marked change in their behavior and in their achievement. Youth and families were helped, and the tutors were richly blessed. One young man, a volunteer tutor, sensed a call to the gospel ministry as a result of his involvement in this program. Delinquent youth all over our land could be helped to a new level of life—to Christian living—if enough people care enough to try to correct the causes of delinquency.

There are causes of human suffering that are so broad that they must be a concern of the entire community, or even of the entire nation. Inadequate education lies behind much of the hostility and violence that mar our American society. Public education should have the support of every Christian. Where there is weakness we should try to provide strength.

The support of Christians is needed also on the side of well-conceived public programs of assistance to the needy. We have seen programs which were poorly planned or poorly managed or badly abused. This does not eliminate the need for assistance programs, and it does not relieve the Christian of responsibility to the unfortunate. Too often Baptists have hidden behind the separation of church and state doctrine to keep free of such programs. I have the conviction that a Christian shows his faith by supporting not only the ministry programs of his church and denomination, but by supporting public programs which seek to deal with such massive national problems as poverty, health, housing and unemployment.

It is encouraging to observe that missionaries and the people with whom they work have undergirded community and national programs in many places.

A few years ago the Central Baptist Church of Oklahoma City made its church facilities available to the Public Health Service. In this way Central church, composed largely of Indians, became a vehicle for a needed health care service to the people of the community which it served. For several years the Chelsea Baptist Church, a mission congregation in a Boston suburb, has rented a portion of its building to the Inter-City Community Action Program.

A list of community service posts held by home missionaries is surprising because of its length. It is encouraging because of the Christian influence these workers have exerted. Here are some of the community positions filled by missionaries during the past few years:

member, President's Council on Indian Problems;
member, state governor's committee on religion;
chaplain, state senate
town mayor;
member, public school board;
member, committee to improve high school education on an Indian reservation;
member, committee on racial problems of city school district;
member, executive committee and board of directors, county youth center;
chairman, community action board;
member, committee to improve Indian-Anglo relationships;
member, city planning board;
consultant, city planning board;
member, city housing committee;
chairman, public housing board for Indians;
member, Model Cities board;
member, committee on drug abuse among Indians;
member, committee to assist in employment of deaf persons.

A host of Baptists in college and seminary today are eager to see the influence of churches count more in dealing with public problems. Their force will be felt increasingly in the years ahead. Seemingly a growing number of adults agree.

It is expected that churches and mission groups, and the ministries of the Home Mission Board, will provide increasing Christian support for worthy public programs. This can be done without compromise of the constitutional guarantees of freedom of worship. This can be done at the same time that local churches and the denomination become more deeply involved in ministering to the disadvantaged. This will not weaken our witness; it will strengthen it.

Future home missions programs may well give more attention to efforts which point directly at helping provide basic human needs. We have already seen some of this in such undertakings as T.O.N.E. (Total Operations for Neighborhood Environment, Inc.). This is a non-profit corporation formed by concerned Southern Baptists of metropolitan New York City. Its purpose is to help people in low income areas find adequate housing, together with needed community facilities.

Their descriptive brochure states: "While T.O.N.E. is upgrading the quality of the building, an intimately coordinated social ministry will be provided by local churches in cooperation with the Metropolitan New York Baptist Association (Southern Baptist)." Their first undertaking was a resounding success. It involved the purchase of a 53-apartment building in Brooklyn, described as "a house without hope." A bank loan which was underwritten by individuals and two Southern Baptist churches, one in New Jersey and one in Texas, made the purchase possible at $67,500. A year later a news story reported: "Today, 24 Furman Avenue is transformed, regenerated, redeemed, a house to which hope has returned."

Such efforts constitute an ounce of prevention in the name of Christ, which God can use to further his purposes for mankind. Look for more of it tomorrow.

Training for Mission

Added emphasis will be given to training volunteer workers, as well as missionaries. During the past decade the response of laypersons has been so great that a change has been made in the annual Home Mission Conferences at Ridgecrest and Glorieta. Agendas have been restructured to provide more classes for the training of laypersons in volunteer mission ministries.

The response in lay witnessing has been phenomenal. This is surely one of the human factors in Southern Baptists' high level of baptisms during the early 1970s. Not only have thousands of laypersons received this training, but a corps of more than 1,000 key lay workers has been trained to conduct church and associational lay witnessing schools.

Hundreds of high school youth have participated in Super Summer training courses lasting more than two weeks. College students across the nation have participated in student evangelism training groups. The Board's renewal evangelism emphasis, now four years old, has likewise been received in an outstanding way. Several hundred lay workers are involved in this ministry of deepening the spiritual lives of church members.

Lay learners' institutes and other training opportunities in the field of interfaith witness have been received enthusiastically. They guide in understanding and witnessing to persons of non-Christian and semi-Christian beliefs. The need for such training is expected to continue. There is no end in sight to the parade of unusual religious views which have appeared in recent years. Such persons as Satan worshippers and gurus from India have pointed up our need for information and training.

A new thing on the horizon is the Urban Training

Cooperative. This is a joint project with the six Southern Baptist seminaries, developed under the leadership of the Home Mission Board's metropolitan missions program. This training plan helps Baptist leaders understand urban structures and discover ways of serving Christ fruitfully in their settings. It is structured in four-day conferences at different cities. Its brightest days surely lie ahead.

The Board's work with minority ethnic peoples is an area where the training of indigenous leaders is essential. The Mexican Baptist Bible Institute in San Antonio, founded and operated by the Baptist General Convention of Texas, has made major contributions to the training of leaders for Spanish language-culture people. The Board joins the Texas convention in providing financial help through sharing in the salaries of the institute's president and six faculty members.

The training of Navajo Indian leaders is considered the chief human factor in the rapid progress of the work with that large Indian tribe in the Southwest. Jack and Betty Comer in Gallup, New Mexico, are among those who have given major attention to training Indians for ministry to their own people, along with David and Ramona McKenzie, themselves Navajo Indians.

Comer has used a small airplane provided by the Board. He flies to the various centers in his field, counsels with local Indian leaders and encourages them in their work. The Navajo pastors, almost without exception, are lay leaders from among the people. By magnifying the training and equipping of local leaders, one missionary couple can accomplish more through others than perhaps a half dozen Anglo missionary couples could do as pastors.

The number of ethnic lay leaders has grown so remarkably that a new name has been coined for them. They are Messengers of the Word. In early 1974 it was estimated that as many as 1,000 laypersons—men, women, youth—were then serving among ethnic peoples. In 1973, 64 persons were recognized for excellence in training as a part of the work of missionaries Eugene and Marina Wolfe among the Spanish-speaking in Los Angeles. James and Marnelle Bowen provided training for 10 to 12 Pueblo Indian laypersons to work among their own people. This approach, first tested in the western states, has become a basic part of the ministries of missionaries Rafael and Miriam Melian in New Orleans, Dolton and Sarah Haggan in Mississippi, Genus and Carolyn Crenshaw in Florida, James and Helen Goodner in Massachusetts, and James Wright in other parts of New England.

It is likely that by the end of this century, few if any Anglos will be serving as pastors of ethnic churches. Their ministry instead will be chiefly directed to equipping Christian workers to serve their own people.

Churches Without Buildings?

Some thoughtful church leaders of various denominations feel that within 15 years as many as one third of the Christian churches in America will not own buildings. Other equally responsible leaders do not foresee this. While this situation likely will not be the case with Southern Baptists, the high cost of land and buildings has already led some young churches to forego the owning of a building for a long time.

The Bergen Baptist Church of Westwood, New Jersey, now has an attractive, adequate building. But it rented the facilities of a Seventh Day Adventist Church for more than 10 years before it got its first building. A new Southern Baptist church was constituted in Holden, Massachusetts, four years ago in a junior high auditorium. The congregation had rented this facility for its meetings from its start. It had grown to a membership of more than 80 at the time the church was constituted. About two thirds of these were native New Englanders.

The Bronx Baptist Church, New York, rented the vacated buildings of a Lutheran church to initiate its Wake-Eden Chapel, a mission in a challenging new field. The Rolling Hills Baptist Church of Pittsburgh met for years in a rented lodge hall. It grew and ministered well in its community.

From California and Oregon to the Great Lakes states and on to Rhode Island and New York, there are several hundred thriving Baptist churches which had their beginnings in homes and apartments, rented church facilities and school buildings, hotels and YMCAs, community buildings and grange halls, storefronts and shopping centers. The number beginning in homes is growing, as home Bible study fellowships have been formed widely within the past few years.

Others, like the congregation in Black Hawk, South Dakota, started in a portable chapel. A youth group from a Tennessee church helped missionaries A.L. and Jewel Davis of Rapid City conduct a Vacation Bible School in Black Hawk in 1972. The Tennessee church provided funds for the purchase of a lot, a mobile chapel was moved onto the site and a continuing work was begun.

Countless churches across the Convention have two or more congregations meeting in the same church facility. This is the case with the Second-Ponce de Leon Baptist Church of Atlanta. A Spanish-language congregation, largely composed of Cubans, is part of the church and conducts its services in the chapel at regular church hours.

It may be that in the decade ahead satellite

ministries will increase. Through this approach one church meets in two or more places and adapts its activities to the needs of the people in each location.

The Monmouth Baptist Church of Eatonton, New Jersey, itself a young mission congregation in 1967, faced the question of whether to enter into an extensive building program to replace its 65-year-old building, or to embark on a program of missions outreach. The church decided to do both—even though this meant that the church would have to postpone the building of new, much needed facilities. Within five years the church was maintaining four church-type chapels and five mission outreach activities. It also remodeled its sanctuary and educational annex.

Some churches have found that special services outside their buildings are an effective way to touch the lives of people who might not attend a service in the church building. The Vineville Baptist Church of Macon, Georgia, has conducted its Easter services in the city auditorium and presented special musical programs there at other times.

The churches of Maui County Baptist Association (Hawaii) sponsored a Christmas worship service at Whalers Village Shopping Center in historic Lahaina. Youth music groups have undergirded our witness with services in parks and shopping centers all across the nation.

To help meet the building finance needs of churches, the Convention has increased the resources of the Home Mission Board's church loan funds greatly during the past 15 years. The Convention has provided Cooperative Program grants and has expanded the Board's authority to borrow funds for relending to churches. It has authorized the Board to purchase sound church bonds for resale to interested investors. The Board's most valuable church loans service, however, is not dispensing money but guiding churches planning to borrow for new facilities. This is expected to be the case in the years ahead.

It seems that in some cases new buildings have served as status symbols more than as instruments of Christian witness and ministry. We can learn something from many of our vibrant young mission churches. Sometimes they have served where all Christian groups were practically unknown. They have had to major on ministries to people, using whatever facilities they could get. They have not seen church buildings as prestige builders, but as instruments with which to glorify God.

Southern Baptists will continue to establish needed new churches, and many more than during the past few years. They are needed in the states where our work is still relatively new. And they are needed in the growing areas of those states where Southern Baptist work has long been well established. As in the past, missions and churches can begin in whatever facilities can be rented or borrowed. As the group grows and resources increase, the Board should be able to provide even more building finance help than in the past.

Laborers Together

Cooperation with concerned groups is expected to grow. Southern Baptist cooperation will broaden at the associational level and between neighboring associations. There will be, also, a growing awareness of other Baptist denominational bodies, since one or more of these serve in each of the 50 states. In the face of persistent moral and spiritual problems, we also will see Christians of other denominations more clearly as co-workers in accomplishing God's purposes.

The problems of the '60s, extending into the '70s,

have required churches to look hard at what is happening in their metropolitan or rural areas. During the 1960s some of the largest Southern Baptist associations lost almost as many churches as they gained in new congregations. One of the largest actually declined in number of churches. We can no longer afford to be satisfied with the progress of our own congregation when our witness in the whole city or area is declining or struggling to keep up.

The four Southern Baptist churches in Milwaukee set an inspiring example in 1973. They united in studying needs of people in the inner city and looked toward working together to meet these needs.

In some cities, strong suburban or downtown churches help support struggling, but needed, churches in the inner city. Some do it by direct grant. Some do it by strong support of the associational mission program. Some operate mission projects in these areas, among minority peoples and needy Anglos. However we may get at it, the future calls for our churches to be truly involved in the welfare of their struggling sister churches.

The years ahead will see an increasing coalition of associations which serve in a given metropolitan area. Within recent years this has happened in such areas as Atlanta, Kansas City, Houston and Los Angeles. Representatives of the four to seven associations which serve within these metropolitan areas have conducted joint meetings, planned and worked together to make an impact on the growing metropolis.

Since the North American Baptist Fellowship was formed 12 years ago, the nine Baptist bodies which participate have become more aware and more appreciative of one another. The fellowship includes not only American Baptist Churches, U.S.A., and the three National Baptist Conventions, but also the North American Baptist General Conference (formerly German Baptist), the Seventh Day Baptist General Conference, the General Association of General Baptists and the Baptist Federation of Canada. This mutual appreciation is expected to increase, extending to other Baptist groups as well. There should be an increasing, though small, number of cooperative projects with one or another of these sister Baptist bodies in the years to come.

During recent years the Home Mission Board has joined with other Baptist and sometimes with non-Baptist groups in specific projects. This was the case in New Haven, Connecticut. A broad program of social ministries imbued with a strong evangelistic purpose was conducted by an organization called Christian Union, Inc.

In the eastern mountains the Home Mission Board has cooperated with several other denominations in an organization called the Commission on Religion in Appalachia.

Just three years ago the Board, through its evangelism development program, led Southern Baptist participation in Key '73, a nationwide, inter-denomination, yearlong evangelistic emphasis.

The military chaplaincy works entirely in an interdenominational setting.

As we look back a quarter of a century, the changes in Southern Baptist home missions are almost un-believable. Missionaries and the Board itself have revised their approaches in many areas. Policies once revered have become obsolete. Methods once productive have been revised or replaced. The attitude of the Board has been one of firmness and flexibility—firmness of purpose and flexibility of method. In times of transition methods likewise must be constantly in transition. That is the story of the decades just past. This must be the story of the years ahead.

AN
EXCITING
TOMORROW

"It is a time for churches to commit themselves afresh to God's will for them. It is a time for bold undertakings in missions."

As we begin the third century of national life, strong waves are pounding against basic moral principles. Concerns for prosperity and pleasure are leading millions to be unconcerned about God and spiritual matters. But this period in our national life also finds more American people searching for spiritual light than perhaps at any other time in history. More are turning to Christ than in years. High school and college youth are especially responsive. The number of adults willing to read and study the Bible has multiplied almost overnight, it seems.

This is a time filled with great opportunities in Christian service. It is a time for churches and members to commit themselves afresh to the will of God for them at this time. It is a time for bold undertakings in missions.

A National Strategy

In the providence of God, Southern Baptists have become the largest evangelical body in the nation. Our foreign missions program encompasses more missionaries in more lands than that of any other evangelical denomination. Our home missions program, it is believed, likewise serves through more missionaries and in more locations than any other denominational homeland missions program.

This furnishes no ground for pride. Rather it is a sobering reminder that Southern Baptists have a heavy responsibility in the shaping of the spiritual and moral life of the United States. The Bicentennial theme, "A Past to Remember—A Future to Mold," speaks to Baptists. Our size, our strength and our nationwide involvement thrust upon us an opportunity and an awesome responsibility.

When the Southern Baptist Convention established its Home Mission Board (then called Domestic Mission Board) the field was small. The entire nation had a population of about 20 million people. Southern Baptist churches were located in states with a combined population of about 7 million. The home missions field in those days included the southern and border states and the western frontier.

Within the past 40 years, the old boundaries have been erased. Southern Baptist work has spilled beyond New Mexico and Arizona to the west. It has moved past Oklahoma and Missouri and Illinois into the midwestern and the north central states. It has spread beyond Kentucky and Virginia and Maryland across the populous northeastern states. The whole nation is our field.

Interestingly, for almost 100 years the Home Mission Board's assignment included two nearby foreign countries, Cuba and Panama. With the return of the last Southern Baptist missionaries from Cuba in 1969 and the termination of the Home Board's responsibilities in Panama in 1975, Southern Baptist home mission fields now consist of the 50 states and the territory of Puerto Rico. This field may expand within the years ahead. Puerto Rican Southern Baptists have shown interest in working in the American-related Virgin Islands, with the support of the Home Mission Board.

As far back as 1959 the Board was directed by the Southern Baptist Convention to give priority to "pioneer" mission fields—state conventions organized since 1940, together with developing areas outside the traditional boundaries of the Convention. The major part of home missionary appointments and financial expenditures go to these fields today, and this will continue.

The Board is concerned also about the older fields.

Many of these have exceptional growth opportunities and in some places, especially cities, a strong challenge to keep from losing ground spiritually.

The northeastern states are prime fields just now. This is a heavily populated, influential region. Work in this area is newer than in any other region and needs maximum help at this stage. The responsiveness of the people is encouraging.

Focus on the Northeast, however, does not mean other parts of the nation stand low on the priority list. For example, six states of the Southwest—New Mexico, Colorado, Arizona, Utah, Nevada and California—are experiencing a prolonged population boom. Fifteen years from now the number of people in these states is expected to be one-third larger, with a combined population of almost 30 million. Texas and Florida are growing rapidly and present inspiring missionary opportunities.

For 30 years California has been a high priority missions field. The same is true of several midwestern, north central and northern plains states where Southern Baptists have served 20 years or more.

California and New York, the two most populous states, have received the largest home missions fund allocations for the past several years. Together they account for almost one fifth of the total population of the United States. A national strategy must continue to give major attention to those fields where large numbers of people are, and where the need for a warmhearted Christian witness is great.

The Home Mission Board's staff and missionaries constantly study such factors as population trends, community changes and religious developments. They join state convention leaders in spotting needs and opportunities. This kind of study, undergirded by divine guidance, helps the Board determine priorities and plan for nationwide efforts.

Home missions stragegy is expected to give major attention to evangelism, new churches and missions, efforts beamed toward all kinds of people, work in the cities, and openness to new ways of touching more people for Christ.

Evangelism.—As the nation enters its third century there are more unchurched people in this land than ever before. There are barriers of culture and color, of economics and education, of religion and respectability which we must cross with the gospel of Christ. The United States is one of the world's most challenging evangelistic fields.

Though the percentage of Americans who are church members is high—over 60 percent—the number of persons who are not affiliated with any Christian body is at least 80 million. And possibly half of the 130 million church members are marginal members, apparently without a deep commitment.

For years Southern Baptists bore their witness in what is called the Bible Belt. Now we are discovering masses of people—both in our southern cities and in our newer fields—who are without a knowledge of the Bible and who have never been closely associated with a church.

Every home missions project aims in some way at helping people to know and follow Jesus Christ. The Board's Evangelism Division seeks to serve churches, associations, state conventions, and all denominational agencies in the effort to keep a faithful Christian witness at the center of our mission to America and the world.

Lay witnesses, both adults and youth, will continue to be a central emphasis in evangelism. Methods may be adjusted and materials revised, but the effort is expected to continue with strength. Renewal evangelism will take on added prominence, in response to the desire of Christians for a deeper experience of Christ and a more effective witness. "Spring Street, USA" is expected to make an increasingly meaningful impact upon the unchurched thousands who view television.

Innovative approaches are anticipated in revival evangelism. Renewed emphasis will be given to the help an association can give churches in evangelism.

Bold new ventures in witnessing will surely appear as compassionate people find ways to communicate the gospel to people without Christ. In the midst of a society marked by many new and sometimes strange lifestyles, the future will call for every Christian to make personal witnessing a part of his personal lifestyle.

New churches and missions.—For years a basic part of the evangelism strategy of Southern Baptists has been to establish new missions, chapels and churches wherever they are needed and wherever they give promise of becoming effective. This must be one of the human reasons for Southern Baptists' continuing growth in membership and churches at a time when most large denominations have declined. And this will certainly continue to be a major item in the denomination's national missions strategy.

Already many of the 33 cooperating state conventions are developing planning for advance in new church starts, after a decade of somewhat small gains.

Two years ago California Southern Baptists launched an effort named "1,006 by '76." This called for a total of 1,006 cooperating churches in that state convention by 1976—a net increase of 90 churches in two years. Arizona is seeking to add 62 churches and missions by 1984, a gain of almost 25 percent. The north central states—Illinois, Indiana, Iowa, Michigan, Minnesota, Ohio and Wisconsin—have planned a joint effort to double all Southern Baptist work in these states by 1990. A major emphasis on new churches would increase the number of Southern Baptist churches in these states from 1,842 to 3,684 during the next 15 years.

Virginia has faced the exciting challenge of its "Urban Corridor"—extending from suburban Washington, D.C., to Norfolk. It set a goal of 58 new churches/missions for that single region. Alabama, Florida, South Carolina and Texas are but some of the strong Baptist conventions which have moved into vigorous new efforts at starting needed missions and churches.

The Home Mission Board is involved in planning with all state conventions. In every case careful attention is given to pinpointing the needs for new work. District associations and local churches are challenged to sponsor new projects, with financial help to come from state conventions and the Home Mission Board as required and available.

Strong emphasis is given to beginning with a home fellowship. The Trinity Baptist Church of Albany, New York, furnishes a shining example of what can be done. Missionary pastor-director J.T. Davis, with missionary Clifford Matthews as church extension director, led their small and scattered congregation to form eight home fellowships within a short time. Three of these soon grew into full-fledged missions and will likely develop into churches. Others ran their course and were discontinued, but gave an evangelistic witness along the way. One of these fellowships led to the conversion of more than eight adults. Much more of this is foreseen all across the country.

In launching their new church drive, California convention executive-secretary Robert D. Hughes stated, "The strongest years of growth came when the spirit of missions outreach burned the brightest. That spirit needs to be recaptured."

His comment points to an important part of the home missions thrust for 1976-79, when the denomination plans its cooperative work around the theme, "Sharing Christ in Bold Mission in a Secular Society." These years of special effort should generate the spiritual momentum essential for another extended period of advance in starting new churches.

All kinds of people.—It is a part of our human nature to feel drawn to people who are "our kind"— people with similar financial resources, vocation, education, attitudes, lifestyles, moral and spiritual standards, and racial, language or cultural backgrounds.

Until recently, people of the southern states, where the bulk of Southern Baptist members reside, lived in a society where the differences from person to person and family to family were not great. Even differences between racial groups were handled in ways generally understood and followed. The generation gap and racial gap existed but they did not normally erupt into confrontations.

We are now at a different point in history, and the southern and western states are filled with people of widely differing viewpoints and backgrounds. The people of these states now face problems encountered in the northern states and the great industrial centers for many years, and they are not conducive to spiritual vitality.

We have always had poor people, but today their needs stand out in dark outline against the background of the living standards of most American people. The very poor are the least "churched" group within the nation.

Ethnic minority peoples have been a significant part of this nation throughout its 200-year history. Today they are more numerous and increasing faster than ever before. Today they are exerting a greater influence upon national policies and the nation's way of life than ever.

Freedom of worship, a basic and precious factor in our national heritage, permits the free exercise and spread of religion. This generation of Americans has seen the appearance of some new and sometimes strange religions. We are observing the heightened vigor and fresh aggressiveness on the part of world religion devotees, such as Buddhists and Moslems.

We have always had our moral failures, people in prisons, and persons released from prison trying to find their way back into respectable society. The pressures of these days exact a high toll as evidenced in our frightening rate of juvenile and adult crime, high suicide rate and alarming number of persons addicted to alcohol and other drugs.

Within the past decade and a half we have become acquainted with "street kids," with youth involved in the drug culture and dabbling with sex, and with young people away from home and hostile toward family and society. We have learned of young people of opposite sexes sharing apartments and of single and married young adults, together with their small children, living together in communes. These are unusual and sometimes repulsive lifestyles to many Christians.

It is true also that sometimes we have as much difficulty loving the prosperous and the respectable as the poor and the moral dropout. We find it as hard to be patient with persons of one's own race, culture and religious heritage as with persons of different racial backgrounds and religious views. We find it as difficult sometimes to feel kindly toward "straight" young people inside our churches as the street kids outside the churches.

The commitment to love all kinds of people will be a fundamental dimension in home missions, as it is now. This commitment will find expression in Home Mission Board policies as the Board sends out missionaries to share Christ with people who follow even the most bizarre and unchristian lifestyles. It will find expression in the Board's willingness to appoint and support missionaries to work among people who cannot be expected to provide the missionary's financial support.

It must send missionaries to people because they are people and because they need Christ. The more confused and troubled and rebellious they are, the more they need Christ, and the more urgent it is to find ways to share the good news of Jesus Christ with them.

This will be the spirit of home missions in seeking to cross barriers of all kinds to bring people of all kinds to know Jesus Christ as Lord.

The commitment to love all people, in obedience to the call and example of Jesus, furnishes a forceful challenge to churches. It is not enough for churches to provide financial support for home missionaries to work with persons in special need. The churches must reach out to all people in need in their respective communities. In some cases a church can involve such people in regular or special activities of the church, such as Bible study, music, weekday ministries, recreation, special classes and clubs. In other cases the best approach will be to establish a special effort aimed at a particular group of people, working alone or with other interested churches, or with the district association.

For the past several years the Eastern Baptist Association (Maryland) has conducted a summer ministry which beautifully expresses compassion for troubled youth and others who frequent the popular Ocean City, Maryland, resort.

As a part of a coordinated inter-church ministry to

beach people, the association's two projects were a hotline emergency telephone service and a coffeehouse. These projects were staffed by the associational missions superintendent and his wife, student summer missionaries, and volunteers from the churches of the association. During the report period there was an average of almost one emergency call an hour, as volunteers manned the phone 24 hours a day, seven days a week.

Calls came from such people as a 15-year-old runaway girl, experimenting with drugs, pregnant, hungry, lonely and frightened. Another call came from the manager of one of the beach's best hotels, asking help for an adult who had taken a large dose of barbituates and washed the pills down with alcohol.

The coffeehouse provided inexpensive short orders plus a 20-minute music program every hour from 9:00 P.M. to 2:00 A.M.

Mike Truitt gave his testimony during one of these periods. The staff had worked with him for three years. The previous summer he had accepted Christ, had broken with drugs and was operating a coffeehouse in Tennessee. Through such personal testimonies, personal conversation and Bible study, the 40 employed and volunteer workers sought to point these youth to Christ for guidance and help.

The cities.—A national missions strategy for the decades ahead must center upon the cities. Whether we think in terms of evangelism or of starting needed new churches, of reaching ethnics or disenchanted youth, it is in the cities that the great needs and opportunities still continue. Our concern is for people, and it is in the cities that the majority of people will be found.

Work in the cities is not easy. It is city people who do most of the moving from one place to another. The recent growth of cities means a high proportion of metropolitan residents have moved there only recently. People such as this do not sink deep roots in the community. Many leave the city on weekends.

Most of Southern Baptists' growth in the pioneer fields has come in the cities. In the main these new churches are in suburban communities of cities such as Tucson, San Diego, Indianapolis and Pittsburgh. There are inner city churches also in these newer areas. You will find Southern Baptist churches ministering in old, depressed communities in downtown philadelphia and inner city Omaha, in Gary, Indiana, and Salt Lake City.

One of the problems of the cities relates to churches in the inner city. More than 2,000 Southern Baptist churches are located in this kind of field, and several hundred have already moved or merged or died. In late 1973 the Board's metropolitan missions program leaders conducted a conference called "Communities in Crisis." It dealt head-on with the problems of change which these churches face. A pastor among the 58 persons who attended the conference wrote in part:

> *After spending a week in the conference . . . I am persuaded that the 2,056 churches in the SBC that are ministering to these communities are in the real forefront of what God is proposing to do in this fast-changing world of today. . . . Even though there is need for financial help in many of these churches, perhaps the greatest need is that our denomination in general be willing to give the same measure of recognition to these churches for the excellent job they are doing as it gives to the churches that enjoy economic and other resource prosperity.*

Plans for the cities require self-studies by associations in metropolitan areas. The Greater Detroit

Baptist Association, for example, made a careful analysis of its entire area and came up with a strategy plan for 1974, 1975 and 1976. Item one in their list of priorities expressed the need "to assist the churches in becoming truly indigenous fellowships whose ministries are directly related to the people whom they ought to serve." A growing number of associations will be gaining a new sense of purpose and direction by conducting the same kind of study.

In some associations the primary need will be to identify and provide appropriate help and encouragement to churches undergoing economic, racial and other social changes.

Two years ago the Birmingham (Alabama) Association faced up to this need and appointed an inner city committee. Within a short time, program help and financial help were on the way for the South Park Baptist Church, located in a changing community. Combined financial help from the association, the state convention and the Home Mission Board was augmented by a contribution from one of the city's strong suburban churches. The South Park church found new encouragement in maintaining its ministry. It embarked upon a diligent effort to minister to its community.

In practically every metropolitan association there are pressing needs to begin well-located, well-staffed churches. This is true in states where Baptist work is strong. In almost every one of these states, Southern Baptists did not start new churches in the 1965-1975 decade as fast as the population increased.

There is urgent need to develop the young churches started a few years ago. But tomorrow's strategy must include also a renewed emphasis on starting churches in all kinds of communities.

At mid-1974 there was at least one Southern Baptist church in all but 11 metropolitan areas with a population of 50,000 or more. Three of these cities have from 200,000 to 400,000 population, the rest from 50,000 to 200,000. At that time there was some kind of mission project in six of these 11, including the three largest cities. All of the 11 cities are in states where Southern Baptist work is relatively new, nine in the Northeast and two in the north central states. Within the near future Southern Baptists should have at least one church in every United States city of 50,000 or more.

We anticipate also a continued maturing of the young chuches. We expect an advance in organizing new churches throughout the so-called pioneer home missions fields of our nation. Many of the expected new churches will consist largely of minority ethnic peoples. Many such people seem to be looking to Southern Baptists for help in establishing an evangelical Christian witness among their peoples.

Our future evangelistic efforts, whether in the form of lay witness, lay renewal or crusade evangelism, must give major attention to the cities. The personal witness of laypersons will be fundamental to any effective effort to claim these metropolitan areas for Christ.

Flexibility.—The Home Mission Board will keep encouraging missionaries and churches to find new ways to reach the unreached with the gospel. The traditional methods continue to be effective in thousands of situations, and in this we rejoice. But even in those churches and mission stations where people respond in large numbers to sermons, music, Bible study, training and prayer fellowship, there are hosts of people untouched by the gospel.

A careful evaluation of almost any church field will likely show that there were more people attending no church on the previous Sunday than the number attending. We rejoice in the large number who participate in church services, but we must ask about the still larger number who do not attend anywhere. It is at this point that innovative efforts are encouraged.

One example of unusual approaches to reaching people was related in a 1974 Baptist Press news story. It told of the relatively small band of Southern Baptists in Metropolitan New York Baptist Association who use their association building facilities to carry on varied and compassionate ministry.

The association, led by missionary Ken Lyle, occupies a six-story office building on West 72nd Street, New York City. Four language groups hold meetings in the building—Spanish, Japanese, Haitian (French speaking), and English. A ministry with Rumanians and Mandarin Chinese was planned. The English-speaking Manhattan Baptist Church, mother church of Southern Baptist work in the metropolitan area and New England, likewise uses these facilities.

A music and drama group and literacy classes were already active, and plans were being projected for a 24-hour telephone counseling service, staffed by retired lay volunteers.

Imaginative programs such as these, inspired by Christian compassion for people, point a finger in the direction of the kind of flexibility and creativity which will continue to permeate home missions strategy.

Missionaries for the Future

The vocational missionary has played an important role in home missions ever since the pioneer preachers carried the gospel to western frontiers. The more subtle, and possibly more difficult, spiritual and moral frontiers before us will call for more missionaries. New and pressing appeals for help come regularly. They call for help in the ghettoes of our southern cities, for assistance to churches struggling with the octopus of community transition, for help in ministering to apartment residents or to persons in resort settings. Then in the newer areas, especially from the north central states through the Northeast, opportunities for new churches and inner city ministries open faster than the Board can respond. Urgent unmet needs demand help in the West as well.

A student summer missionary, Ann Harrell of Mississippi, wrote a glowing account of her summer's activities in Pennsylvania and western New York. She told of one mission Vacation Bible School held in a tent and another conducted in a little town 13 miles out of Coraopolis, Pennsylvania. In her final written report she thanked the Lord for a wonderful summer and commented: "I think it's a shame that the places that the missionaries work in the summer are left without any kind of witness until the next summer, and sometimes not even then. These people both young and old are so very hungry for God, his Word, and his love."

Strange, isn't it? It sounds like the frontier days when the itinerant preacher came by and preached once a quarter or once a year. But the summer missionary was speaking of today.

Dozens of missionaries will be needed. Couples and single people will be welcomed in Christian social ministries.

Specialists will be needed in such work as starting new churches, planning and conducting weekday community ministries, and the leading and training of others for ministries such as those performed by Messengers of the Word. If funds are available, the missionary force could be increased by 200 a year—a figure we have not reached in several years—and still leave as many unanswered calls as we had answered.

The need for chaplains will change. The expected years of peace after our withdrawal from Indochina will reduce our nation's standing military forces. This will cut Southern Baptists' quota of military chaplains and will sharply reduce the opportunities of those desiring to enter the military chaplaincy. On the other hand, a steady if not sharp increase is expected in all areas of civilian chaplaincy.

Growing concern for the rehabilitation of prisoners is expected to increase the number of chaplains needed in such institutions. The industrial chaplaincy is proving to be a valuable ministry in many businesses. A sizeable number of companies are expected to view the ministry of a staff chaplain favorably. More and more private hospitals, and some public, will be placing chaplains on their staffs as they recognize the role of the chaplain on the healing team.

The speed with which calls for missionaries are answered will be determined in large part by the financial support Southern Baptists provide. During the early 1970s the Board's total support increased about 5 percent a year while inflation hiked operational costs by 6 to 10 percent. This requried a cutback of nonpersonnel items in order to help missionaries and staff keep abreast of rising living costs. An increase in total number of missionaries was impossible at that time.

Now we see encouraging advances in Cooperative Program giving. The Annie Armstrong Easter Offering has made strong gains. It is hoped that this growing support, even in the face of rising costs, will provide finances for a missionary force of 2,500 by the end of the 1970s.

The trend toward placing fewer workers with single congregations, other than mission pastors, will gain momentum. Missionaries like Terrell L. Moore in McConnellsville, Ohio, will be expected to serve large sections of a state, beginning and maintaining work in several places as need and opportunity meet.

Some will have assignments like that of Donald and Mary Ann Rollins, who use a small airplane to serve widely scattered settlements from their base in King Salmon, Alaska. There will be a growing number of workers like John and Shirley Hopkins in Kansas City, Kansas, and Robert and Martha Couch in Huntsville, Alabama, who help the churches of an association in establishing ministries related to persons in special need.

There will likely be a greater number of general missionaries with an association or a grouping of ethnic churches. L.A. Watson, who works with an association of Indian churches in Oklahoma, carries this kind of responsibility.

Workers with the deaf will in the main serve as Jerry and Erkle St. John do in Mississippi, training workers and helping churches conduct ministries to deaf persons.

Homeland missions strategy in the years ahead will call for a stepped-up emphasis on equipping others for service. More attention will be given to what the missionary can train others to accomplish than on what she or he can do personally in direct mission activities.

Then there are the exciting two-year responsibilities undertaken by US-2ers. One thinks of recent US-2ers and their work—the campus ministry of Joe and Sally Glaze in College (Fairbanks), Alaska; the work of Jim and Edna Barnes with deaf students in the Harrison-Chilhowee Baptist Academy in Seymour, Tennessee; the music ministry of Gwen Williams in Detroit; and the challenge of developing the first Southern Baptist church in Montpelier, the capital of Vermont, under-taken by Bill and Linda Gaddis.

Doubtless there will be missionary tasks of which no one has yet dreamed. As needs arise and the possibility of a significant Christian witness appears, the Home Mission Board will boldly take on additional experimental ministries.

Whatever the nature of the missionary's responsibility, the demands on these workers will be heavier than ever. The rising educational level of the American people calls for well-trained missionaries. A genuine love for people is fundamental. The willingness and ability to work with others and to work through others will be more important than ever. A firm commitment to Jesus Christ, a life that bears testimony to Christ, and a sense of call to missions are basic in the life of any missionary.

Laypeople in Missions

The Home Mission Board's plans call for an expanding involvement of laypersons in home missions beyond the local church.

A few years ago layman Owen Cooper, then president of the Southern Baptist Convention, threw out a challenge to Southern Baptist mission leaders to enlist 5,000 retired persons in non-salaried mission work. Many retired men and women have had the time of their lives serving as associate missionaries for a month or a summer or a year. Many other adults, not yet retired, have had enriching experiences.

Retiree missions at its best was exemplified by Mr. and Mrs. Dallas McLemore of Gainesville, Texas. At a World Missions Conference they became interested in the work in Wisconsin and Minnesota. For the next four years they served in this two-state field from May until October. The McLemores started new mission work, set up home Bible studies, conducted backyard Bible clubs, helped start a bus ministry, supervised summer missionaries, and introduced others to the knowledge of Jesus Christ.

A few months before his death Mr. McLemore

stated: "We have received more blessings and had more happen in the last four years than any since we've been married."

Whatever one's training may be, there is a place for it. Mr. and Mrs. Bill Crotts of Christiansburg, Virginia, helped construct a home for the missionary family at Teec Nos Pos, New Mexico. Mrs. Madge M. Laws of Cabool, Missouri, used her library skills to organize and process books for the library of the Caney Creek Baptist Church and its weekday ministries.

Mrs. Elesa Straley of Tampa, Florida, used her musical skills in Iowa for two weeks in 1972, and for a similar period in northwestern Nevada the next year. Mrs. Eloise Bean of Kountze, Texas, served six weeks in Michigan in 1968, followed four years later by a three-and-one-half-week stint in New Mexico.

All of these people went at their own expense. All expressed joy and gratitude for the experience. All expressed the hope and desire to go on another such mission. These are a part of what the Home Mission Board calls the Christian Service Corps. They are adult volunteers who go at their own expense and help home missionaries for a limited period of time.

Some Christian Service Corps people use their vocations to get involved in home missions before retirement. This is the case of Mr. and Mrs. Larry Nicholson, formerly of Lilburn, Georgia. They became excited about the possibility of serving in the West. Nicholson sold his plumbing equipment, and the young couple moved to Colorado without employment. He soon found work, and later was employed by Colorado Southern Baptists at their state assembly grounds.

Mr. and Mrs. James Walker from Louisiana followed the same route. Upon graduation from pharmacy school Walker declined a higher paying position closer to home and accepted a position in Baltimore where the couple could serve as part-time volunteer workers in a mission setting.

The number of volunteers is increasing rapidly, and there is a reason. The Christian Service Corps is now directed by a volunteer, himself a Christian Service Corpsman. W.L. "Bill" Wilson, an active layman and church deacon of Decatur, Georgia, was anxious to get more involved in the Lord's work. His business had reached the point that it no longer required his full-time attention. The Board gladly accepted his offer of half-time work without salary. This layman is leading the challenge to mature adults to get involved in short-term, volunteer home missions work.

Then there are campers on mission, appealing to adults and entire families to use their campground and travel experiences to count for Christ. The response has been phenomenal, and further growth is anticipated.

The involvement of more college students in home missions has been an exciting development. The number of summer-long student missionaries remained at the 1,000 a year level in the early 1970s. David Ford of North Carolina, for example, served on an evangelism team in Oregon, using a coffeehouse as a base for witnessing. Gerald L. David of Missouri, serving in a resort missions situation at the Standing Stone Park in Tennessee, had exceptional experiences in his work with troubled young people.

Semester student missions began four years ago as a way for students with free time during the regular school session to be involved in mission projects. It started with six students and is gaining momentum. Hundreds of other students have worked at ski resorts, beach ministries, church building construction, Indian villages and inner city ministries between summers. One such project in the Baltimore area received national television and newspaper coverage.

High school seniors have desired this kind of involvement. Three years ago the Board commissioned a US-2er, Clay Price, to enlist high school graduates or rising seniors to give a summer in home missions work. The first summer 24 high school youth went out under this new Sojourner ministry. Four young people, three from Arkansas and one from Utah, recently gave a full year to home missions at the expense of their families. This extremely promising approach is expected to catch fire within the years just ahead.

Home missions strategy calls for a greatly increased number of youth and adult volunteers:

- 500 adults in short-term Christian Service Corps ministries;
- 15,000 enrolled in Campers on Mission;
- 1,500 college students per year in summer missions, plus 150 in student semester missions;
- 250 high school graduates in Sojourner missions and 50 youth on mission annually at no expense to the Home Mission Board.

Missions is indeed every Christian's business. Exciting levels of service are foreseen as Baptists respond to the challenge of tomorrow.

You Can Make A Difference

The Bicentennial provides time for a fresh thrust in home missions. That advance does not depend on what one or two outstanding persons do or what one or two strong churches do. The strength of Southern Baptist missions programs rests essentially in the fact that a great many people and churches take part. When even half of our 12 million members get involved that is a mighty army! And every person counts.

To mount the kind and size of national missions

effort which the circumstances demand will require rapid increases in financial support. The outlook is encouraging, but it takes more than money to carry on a missions program. It takes prayer as well. Our directions come from God. Power comes from him. He has taught us to pray. He has promised to answer earnest, believing prayer. Even doubled budgets without a vital relationship to God through prayer would be powerless.

But beyond our personal giving and our church's giving, and beyond our praying, is personal commitment. God said, "Blessed is the nation whose God is the Lord." Our personal commitment to Christ, plus the commitment of others, forms a mighty force for good and for the gospel. The dedication we need includes an obedient life of love and service, but it must be larger than this. It must envelop the commitment to make God's mission our mission. It is not his will that any should miss Christ and miss life abundant and life eternal. It is not his will that America should miss God and face the decline that some other nations have experienced.

It is at the point of our commitment that we meet a series of penetrating questions—questions we must face if Baptists are to fulfill their responsibilities under God in the challenging third century of our national life.

• Can we learn to love and appreciate persons as persons regardless of their differences from us in language, culture, race, age, lifestyle, moral and spiritual need?

• Can we—will we—truly major on helping people in the name of Christ, placing "people values" above organizational conformity or numerical concerns or building programs or public prestige?

• Can we—will we—care enough for people and groups who do not produce quick visible results

96

—such as in statistics or finances—to serve them faithfully and gladly?

• Will we take the risks necessary to attempt needed new missionary efforts of an unconventional nature—risks of failure? Risks of misunderstanding and criticism?

• Will we be Christian enough to place the purposes of Christ for this nation and for all nations and peoples above regional, local, cultural and even denominational concerns?

• Will the churches be missionary enough to supply a steady stream of God-called young men and women to enter the ranks of missionaries at work in challenging and difficult fields across our land and around the world?

• Can we respond heartily to Christ's call to share the gospel with the world—the world that includes both one's own community and the rest of the nation and of the world?

It is not so important that we be able to answer yes to all the questions as it is to determine that we will strive to make yes our answer, whatever adjustments may be necessary.

We stand on the threshold of the greatest need and the greatest opportunity for advance in home missions that we have had in our 130 years as a denomination. With God's help can we qualify for his use as an instrument to bring a fresh spiritual awakening to our land and our world? We can—with God's help!

The response of each church will make a difference. Your and my responses will make a difference.

For the sake of America, for the sake of a world that looks to this nation for moral example and spiritual help, this is the time for bold and vigorous advances in rebuilding Christian foundations in our beloved nation. A worthy, Christ-honoring tomorrow must start today.

Questions

Chapter 1
1. Name three challenges facing the SBC and tell what the Home Mission Board is doing to meet them.
2. Name at least two of the new missions frontiers.
3. How are some churches and missionaries ministering on the new frontiers?
4. Define a "new town" and name the HMB's national new town consultant.
5. Rutledge says, "The spiritual frontiers of today come to sharpest focus in the cities." Why is this true?

Chapter 2
1. How is the HMB using new communication methods to cross barriers?
2. Name some cooperative efforts between the HMB and state conventions in resort area missions.
3. What is Campers on Mission?
4. The mobile American is creating problems for churches and missionaries. Why? What can you do in your community to reach people on the move? What is the HMB doing to relate to the mobile American?
5. Name some ways you and your church can support home missions efforts.

Chapter 3
1. Rutledge says the Board will probably not appoint missionaries to major on work with the aging. What will the Board do to minister to this segment of our population?
2. What is the HMB's new approach to migrant ministry?
3. Name three categories by which home missionaries seek to meet the needs of the disadvantaged. What are the means for meeting each of these needs?
4. Rutledge predicts that the number of language missionaries will decrease in future years. Why?
5. What is the Board's viewpoint on providing help to minority groups so that they may minister to their own?

Chapter 4
1. Name at least four new approaches to reaching Christless people.
2. What is meant by the statement, "The power is in the gospel, not in methods"?
3. How can churches fill the vacuum created by what Rutledge terms "the loss of a sense of neighborhood"? What can your church do in your community?
4. Name at least five groups with whom the HMB may establish specific ministries in the near future. Suggest ways of ministering to these groups.
5. Rutledge predicts that by the end of this century, few if any Anglos will be serving as pastors of ethnic churches. Why does he predict this?

Chapter 5
1. How does the HMB determine priorities and plan nationwide efforts?
2. Name the five thrusts of future home missions strategy.
3. Rutledge says "the commitment to love all kinds of people will be a fundamental dimension in home missions . . ." Name two ways this commitment will find expression.
4. Churches are exhorted to "reach out to all people in need in their respective communities." Using the suggestions on the bottom of page 83, suggest specific ways your church can reach out in your community.
5. Name five missions opportunities for laypersons. Which one fits you?

NOTES

1. Quoted by Edward B. Lindaman, "What Life Will Be Like in the 70's," *Review and Expositor,* vol. LXVII, no. 1, Winter, 1970, p. 16. The second line of the quote has supplied the title of this book.
2. Ronald Schiller, "America's Dying Small Towns: Tragedy or Opportunity?," condensed from *National Civic Review, Reader's Digest,* July, 1972, p. 201.
3. *U.S. News & World Report,* February 25, 1974.
4. Will Herberg, "Religion in the U.S.—Where it's Headed," *U.S. News & World Report,* vol. LXXIV, no. 23, June 4, 1973, pp. 54-60.

ABOUT THE AUTHOR . . .

Arthur B. Rutledge, executive director-treasurer of the Home Mission Board since 1965, is a familiar personality to Baptists. His dedication and leadership have been recognized many times. In 1973, he received the Christian Life Commission's Distinguished Service Award.

Before becoming the Board's chief executive, Rutledge served six years as director of the Division of Missions, HMB. He came to Atlanta from Texas, where he served as director of missions for the Texas convention. He served 25 years as pastor in that state and in Indiana.

Rutledge is a graduate of Baylor University, Southern Baptist Theological Seminary and Southwestern Baptist Theological Seminary. He holds honorary doctor's degrees from East Texas Baptist College and Baylor University.